ORGAN
TRANSPLANTS

GENERAL EDITORS

Dale C. Garell, M.D.
Medical Director, California Children Services, Department of Health
    Services, County of Los Angeles
Clinical Professor, Department of Pediatrics & Family Medicine,
    University of Southern California School of Medicine
Former president, Society for Adolescent Medicine

Solomon H. Snyder, M.D.
Distinguished Service Professor of Neuroscience, Pharmacology, and
    Psychiatry, Johns Hopkins University School of Medicine
Former president, Society of Neuroscience
Albert Lasker Award in Medical Research, 1978

CONSULTING EDITORS

Robert W. Blum, M.D., Ph.D.
Associate Professor, School of Public Health and Department of
    Pediatrics
Director, Adolescent Health Program, University of Minnesota
Consultant, World Health Organization

Charles E. Irwin, Jr., M.D.
Associate Professor of Pediatrics
Director, Division of Adolescent Medicine,
    University of California, San Francisco

Lloyd J. Kolbe, Ph.D.
Chief, Office of School Health & Special Projects, Center for Health
    Promotion & Education, Centers for Disease Control
President, American School Health Association

Jordan J. Popkin
Director, Division of Federal Employee Occupational Health, U.S. Public
    Health Service Region I

Joseph L. Rauh, M.D.
Professor of Pediatrics and Medicine, Adolescent Medicine, Children's
    Hospital Medical Center, Cincinnati
Former president, Society for Adolescent Medicine

THE ENCYCLOPEDIA OF
H E A L T H

THE HEALTHY BODY

Dale C. Garell, M.D. · General Editor

ORGAN TRANSPLANTS

Mary Kittredge

Introduction by C. Everett Koop, M.D., Sc.D.

Surgeon General, U.S. Public Health Service

CHELSEA HOUSE PUBLISHERS

New York   Philadelphia

ON THE COVER: Photo courtesy of Stanford University Medical Center

Chelsea House Publishers
EDITOR-IN-CHIEF: Nancy Toff
EXECUTIVE EDITOR: Remmel T. Nunn
MANAGING EDITOR: Karyn Gullen Browne
COPY CHIEF: Juliann Barbato
PICTURE EDITOR: Adrian G. Allen
ART DIRECTOR: Maria Epes
MANUFACTURING MANAGER: Gerald Levine

The Encyclopedia of Health
SENIOR EDITOR: Jane Larkin Crain

Staff for ORGAN TRANSPLANTS
ASSISTANT EDITOR: Laura Dolce
COPY EDITOR: Terrance Dolan
DEPUTY COPY CHIEF: Ellen Scordato
EDITORIAL ASSISTANT: Susan DeRosa
PICTURE RESEARCHER: Debra Hershkowitz
DESIGNER: Victoria Tomaselli
ASSISTANT DESIGNER: Donna Sinisgalli
PRODUCTION COORDINATOR: Joseph Romano

First Printing

1   3   5   7   9   8   6   4   2

Library of Congress Cataloging in Publication Data
Kittredge, Mary, 1949–
    Organ transplants / Mary Kittredge.
        p.   cm.—(The Encyclopedia of health)
    Bibliography: p.
    Includes index.
    Summary: discusses the progress made in the field of organ
transplants, how and to whom the process is done, and the ethical questions trans-
plants raise.
RD120.76.K58   1988   617'.95—dc19   88-14098
ISBN 0-7910-0071-0   CIP
       0-7910-0498-8 (pbk.)   AC

CONTENTS

Prevention and Education: The Keys to Good Health—
C. Everett Koop, M.D., Sc.D. 7

Foreword—Dale C. Garrell, M.D. 9

Author's Preface: Organ Transplants 13

1 Organ Transplants Then and Now 17

2 Which Organs—And Why? 27

3 The Perfect Match 39

4 The Body Vigilant 47

How a Heart Transplant Happens. 55

5 A Patient's Point of View 61

6 Ethical Issues 75

7 The Future of Organ Transplantation 87

Appendix 1: For More Information 93

Appendix 2: How to Become an Organ Donor 96

Further Reading 97

Glossary 98

Index 103

THE HEALTHY BODY

The Circulatory System
Dental Health
The Digestive System
The Endocrine System
Exercise
Genetics & Heredity
The Human Body: An Overview
Hygiene
The Immune System
Memory & Learning
The Musculoskeletal System
The Neurological System
Nutrition
The Reproductive System
The Respiratory System
The Senses
Speech & Hearing
Sports Medicine
Vision
Vitamins & Minerals

THE LIFE CYCLE

Adolescence
Adulthood
Aging
Childhood
Death & Dying
The Family
Friendship & Love
Pregnancy & Birth

MEDICAL ISSUES

Careers in Health Care
Environmental Health
Folk Medicine
Health Care Delivery
Holistic Medicine
Medical Ethics
Medical Fakes & Frauds
Medical Technology
Medicine & the Law
Occupational Health
Public Health

PSYCHOLOGICAL DISORDERS AND THEIR TREATMENT

Anxiety & Phobias
Child Abuse
Compulsive Behavior
Delinquency & Criminal Behavior
Depression
Diagnosing & Treating Mental Illness
Eating Habits & Disorders
Learning Disabilities
Mental Retardation
Personality Disorders
Schizophrenia
Stress Management
Suicide

MEDICAL DISORDERS AND THEIR TREATMENT

AIDS
Allergies
Alzheimer's Disease
Arthritis
Birth Defects
Cancer
The Common Cold
Diabetes
Drugs: Prescription & OTC
First Aid & Emergency Medicine
Gynecological Disorders
Headaches
The Hospital
Kidney Disorders
Medical Diagnosis
The Mind-Body Connection
Mononucleosis & Other Infectious Diseases
Nuclear Medicine
Organ Transplants
Pain
Physical Handicaps
Poisons & Toxins
Sexually Transmitted Diseases
Skin Diseases
Stroke & Heart Disease
Substance Abuse
Tropical Medicine

PREVENTION AND EDUCATION: THE KEYS TO GOOD HEALTH

C. Everett Koop, M.D., Sc.D.
Surgeon General,
U.S. Public Health Service

The issue of health education has received particular attention in recent years because of the presence of AIDS in the news. But our response to this particular tragedy points up a number of broader issues that doctors, public health officials, educators, and the public face. In particular, it points up the necessity for sound health education for citizens of all ages.

Over the past 25 years this country has been able to bring about dramatic declines in the death rates for heart disease, stroke, accidents, and, for people under the age of 45, cancer. Today, Americans generally eat better and take better care of themselves than ever before. Thus, with the help of modern science and technology, they have a better chance of surviving serious—even catastrophic—illnesses. That's the good news.

But, like every phonograph record, there's a flip side, and one with special significance for young adults. According to a report issued in 1979 by Dr. Julius Richmond, my predecessor as Surgeon General, Americans aged 15 to 24 had a higher death rate in 1979 than they did 20 years earlier. The causes: violent death and injury, alcohol and drug abuse, unwanted pregnancies, and sexually transmitted diseases. Adolescents are particularly vulnerable, because they are beginning to explore their own sexuality and perhaps to experiment with drugs. The need for educating young people is critical, and the price of neglect is high.

Yet even for the population as a whole, our health is still far from what it could be. Why? A 1974 Canadian government report attributed all death and disease to four broad elements: inadequacies in the health-care system, behavioral factors or unhealthy life-styles, environmental hazards, and human biological factors.

To be sure, there are diseases that are still beyond the control of even our advanced medical knowledge and techniques. And despite yearnings that are as old as the human race itself, there is no "fountain of youth" to ward off aging and death. Still, there is a solution to many of the problems that undermine sound health. In a word, that solution is prevention. Prevention, which includes health promotion and education, saves lives, improves the quality of life, and, in the long run, saves money.

In the United States, organized public health activities and preventive medicine have a long history. Important milestones include the improvement of sanitary procedures and the development of pasteurized milk in the late 19th century, and the introduction in the mid-20th century of effective vaccines against polio, measles, German measles, mumps, and other once-rampant diseases. Internationally, organized public health efforts began on a wide-scale basis with the International Sanitary Conference of 1851, to which 12 nations sent representatives. The World Health Organization, founded in 1948, continues these efforts under the aegis of the United Nations, with particular emphasis on combatting communicable diseases and the training of health-care workers.

But despite these accomplishments, much remains to be done in the field of prevention. For too long, we have had a medical care system that is science- and technology-based, focused, essentially, on illness and mortality. It is now patently obvious that both the social and the economic costs of such a system are becoming insupportable.

Implementing prevention—and its corollaries, health education and promotion—is the job of several groups of people:

First, the medical and scientific professions need to continue basic scientific research, and here we are making considerable progress. But increased concern with prevention will also have a decided impact on how primary-care doctors practice medicine. With a shift to health-based rather than morbidity-based medicine, the role of the "new physician" will include a healthy dose of patient education.

Second, practitioners of the social and behavioral sciences—psychologists, economists, city planners—along with lawyers, business leaders, and government officials—must solve the practical and ethical dilemmas confronting us: poverty, crime, civil rights, literacy, education, employment, housing, sanitation, environmental protection, health care delivery systems, and so forth. All of these issues affect public health.

Third is the public at large. We'll consider that very important group in a moment.

Fourth, and the linchpin in this effort, is the public health profession—doctors, epidemiologists, teachers—who must harness the professional expertise of the first two groups and the common sense and cooperation of the third, the public. They must define the problems statistically and qualitatively and then help us set priorities for finding the solutions.

To a very large extent, improving those statistics is the responsibility of every individual. So let's consider more specifically what the role of the individual should be and why health education is so important to that role. First, and most obviously, individuals can protect themselves from illness and injury and thus minimize their need for professional medical care. They can eat a nutritious diet, get adequate exercise, avoid tobacco, alcohol, and drugs, and take prudent steps to avoid accidents. The proverbial "apple a day keeps the doctor away" is not so far from the truth, after all.

Second, individuals should actively participate in their own medical care. They should schedule regular medical and dental checkups. Should they develop an illness or injury, they should know when to treat themselves and when to seek professional help. To gain the maximum benefit from any medical treatment that they do require, individuals must become partners in that treatment. For instance, they should understand the effects and side effects of medications. I counsel young physicians that there is no such thing as too much information when talking with patients. But the corollary is the patient must know enough about the nuts and bolts of the healing process to understand what the doctor is telling him. That is at least partially the patient's responsibility.

Education is equally necessary for us to understand the ethical and public policy issues in health care today. Sometimes individuals will encounter these issues in making decisions about their own treatment or that of family members. Other citizens may encounter them as jurors in medical malpractice cases. But we all become involved, indirectly, when we elect our public officials, from school board members to the president. Should surrogate parenting be legal? To what extent is drug testing desirable, legal, or necessary? Should there be public funding for family planning, hospitals, various types of medical research, and medical care for the indigent? How should we allocate scant technological resources, such as kidney dialysis and organ transplants? What is the proper role of government in protecting the rights of patients?

What are the broad goals of public health in the United States today? In 1980, the Public Health Service issued a report aptly entitled *Promoting Health-Preventing Disease: Objectives for the Nation.*This report expressed its goals in terms of mortality and in terms of intermediate goals in education and health improvement. It identified 15 major concerns: controlling high blood pressure; improving family planning; improving pregnancy care and infant health; increasing the rate of immunization; controlling sexually transmitted diseases; controlling the presence of toxic agents and radiation in the environment; improving occupational safety and health; preventing accidents; promoting water fluoridation and dental health; controlling infectious diseases; decreasing smoking; decreasing alcohol and drug abuse; improving nutrition; promoting physical fitness and exercise; and controlling stress and violent behavior.

For healthy adolescents and young adults (ages 15 to 24), the specific goal was a 20% reduction in deaths, with a special focus on motor vehicle injuries and alcohol and drug abuse. For adults (ages 25 to 64), the aim was 25% fewer deaths, with a concentration on heart attacks, strokes, and cancers.

Smoking is perhaps the best example of how individual behavior can have a direct impact on health. Today cigarette smoking is recognized as the most important single preventable cause of death in our society. It is responsible for more cancers and more cancer deaths than any other known agent; is a prime risk factor for heart and blood vessel disease, chronic bronchitis, and emphysema; and is a frequent cause of complications in pregnancies and of babies born prematurely, underweight, or with potentially fatal respiratory and cardiovascular problems.

Since the release of the Surgeon General's first report on smoking in 1964, the proportion of adult smokers has declined substantially, from 43% in 1965 to 30.5% in 1985. Since 1965, 37 million people have quit smoking. Although there is still much work to be done if we are to become a "smoke-free society," it is heartening to note that public health and public education efforts—such as warnings on cigarette packages and bans on broadcast advertising—have already had significant effects.

In 1835, Alexis de Tocqueville, a French visitor to America, wrote, "In America the passion for physical well-being is general." Today, as then, health and fitness are front-page items. But with the greater scientific and technological resources now available to us, we are in a far stronger position to make good health care available to everyone. And with the greater technological threats to us as we approach the 21st century, the need to do so is more urgent than ever before. Comprehensive information about basic biology, preventive medicine, medical and surgical treatments, and related ethical and public policy issues can help you arm yourself with the knowledge you need to be healthy throughout your life.

FOREWORD

Dale C. Garell, M.D.

Advances in our understanding of health and disease during the 20th century have been truly remarkable. Indeed, it could be argued that modern health care is one of the greatest accomplishments in all of human history. In the early 1900s, improvements in sanitation, water treatment, and sewage disposal reduced death rates and increased longevity. Previously untreatable illnesses can now be managed with antibiotics, immunizations, and modern surgical techniques. Discoveries in the fields of immunology, genetic diagnosis, and organ transplantation are revolutionizing the prevention and treatment of disease. Modern medicine is even making inroads against cancer and heart disease, two of the leading causes of death in the United States.

Although there is much to be proud of, medicine continues to face enormous challenges. Science has vanquished diseases such as smallpox and polio, but new killers, most notably AIDS, confront us. Moreover, we now victimize ourselves with what some have called "diseases of choice," or those brought on by drug and alcohol abuse, bad eating habits, and mismanagement of the stresses and strains of contemporary life. The very technology that is doing so much to prolong life has brought with it previously unimaginable ethical dilemmas related to issues of death and dying. The rising cost of health-care is a matter of central concern to us all. And violence in the form of automobile accidents, homicide, and suicide remain the major killers of young adults.

In the past, most people were content to leave health care and medical treatment in the hands of professionals. But since the 1960s, the consumer of medical care—that is, the patient—has assumed an increasingly central role in the management of his or her own health. There has also been a new emphasis placed on prevention: People are recognizing that their own actions can help prevent many of the conditions that have caused death and disease in the past. This accounts for the growing commitment to good nutrition and regular exercise, for the fact that more and more people are choosing not to smoke, and for a new moderation in people's drinking habits.

People want to know more about themselves and their own health. They are curious about their body: its anatomy, physiology, and biochemistry. They want to keep up with rapidly evolving medical technologies and procedures. They are willing to educate themselves about common disorders and diseases so that they can be full partners in their own health-care.

The ENCYCLOPEDIA OF HEALTH is designed to provide the basic knowledge that readers will need if they are to take significant responsibility for their own health. It is also meant to serve as a frame of reference for further study and exploration. The ENCYCLOPEDIA is divided into five subsections: The Healthy Body; The Life Cycle; Medical Disorders & Their Treatment; Psychological Disorders & Their Treatment; and Medical Issues. For each topic covered by the ENCYCLOPEDIA, we present the essential facts about the relevant biology; the symptoms, diagnosis, and treatment of common diseases and disorders; and ways in which you can prevent or reduce the severity of health problems when that is possible. The ENCYCLOPEDIA also projects what may lie ahead in the way of future treatment or prevention strategies.

The broad range of topics and issues covered in the ENCYCLOPEDIA reflects the fact that human health encompasses physical, psychological, social, environmental, and spiritual well-being. Just as the mind and the body are inextricably linked, so, too, is the individual an integral part of the wider world that comprises his or her family, society, and environment. To discuss health in its broadest aspect it is necessary to explore the many ways in which it is connected to such fields as law, social science, public policy, economics, and even religion. And so, the ENCYCLOPEDIA is meant to be a bridge between science, medical technology, the world at large, and you. I hope that it will inspire you to pursue in greater depth particular areas of interest, and that you will take advantage of the suggestions for further reading and the lists of resources and organizations that can provide additional information.

· · · · · · · · · · · · · · ·

ORGAN TRANSPLANTS

Dr. Christiaan Barnard

U ntil the early 1950s, organ transplants belonged more to the realm of science fiction than to medical science. Eye banks had been operating since the 1940s, but it was not until the early 1950s, when kidney transplants were first attempted, that the general public began to accept the concept of organ transplants as a reality. Kidney transplants were, in earlier years, successful only under very special conditions. Now, in 1986 alone, more than 8,000 people in the United States—including hundreds of teenagers—received new kidneys and a new lease on life. More than 85% of the new kidneys, and close to 95% of the patients in some cases, survive the first year. And of those patients who reject their donated kidney, many receive a second chance at transplant.

The first human heart transplant was performed in 1967, in Cape Town, South Africa, when Dr. Christiaan Barnard transplanted the heart of a young accident victim, Denise Darvall, into the body of 55-year-old Louis Washkansky. In 1968, Dr. Norman E. Shumway performed the first heart transplant done in the United States, at Stanford University Medical Center in California. More than a decade later, however, heart transplants were still rare occurrences. In 1981 62 heart-transplant operations were performed in the United States, and the 1-year survival rate was only 67%.

But today, this and many other kinds of organ transplant surgery are becoming more commonplace. Although the first heart transplant patients survived for only days or months, more than 80% of such patients now live at least a year after surgery. In 1986, more than 1,300 heart transplants were performed in the United States; in 1987, one of the longest-living transplant patients celebrated the 15th year of life with his new heart.

Liver transplant, long thought to be especially risky, is now successful more than 65% of the time. One of the longest living liver transplant patients is now 20 years old; she received her new liver when she was 4. Even transplants considered to be extremely difficult are being done more frequently and successfully. In 1986, for example, 50 patients received heart-lung transplants; nearly 70% of the patients undergoing this surgery now survive for a year or more. One patient who received both a heart and a lung transplant in 1985 is still alive.

Organ transplants have not only extended the life of many chronically ill patients but have also greatly improved the quality of their life as well. In 1984, for example, more than 24,000 people regained sight through corneal transplants (replacement of the clear covering of the eye). Bone transplants can save arms and legs that would previously have had to be amputated. Kidney transplants have given unknown freedom to many people who were formerly forced to undergo dialysis several times week.

Nor are "real" organs the only ones that can be used to improve and save lives. Better hearing, regular heartbeats, and even the ability to breathe may be restored by implants: synthetic body parts made of plastics or metal. The most dramatic of these is, of course, the artificial heart, the use of which is still in the experimental stages.

Another implant now being used is the insulin pump. Implanted in the body of diabetics, the pump dispenses regular doses of insulin (a substance the body uses in digesting sugar) thus eliminating the need for frequent injections.

The past three decades have witnessed great medical advances in the field of organ transplants and implants. Although we are not yet able to create the "bionic human," we have made revolutionary progress in the development of ever more sophisticated surgical techniques and artificial organs. Lifesaving feats of which our grandparents only dreamed are now being performed every day.

How did it happen? What changed organ-transplant surgery from a dangerous experiment into a technique so common that it is now, in some cases, almost routine? And what does this progress mean to each of us? What new benefits will we enjoy, and what new problems will we be asked to solve in this dawning age of successful organ transplants?

It has often been said that with each new freedom comes a new responsibility, and this can also be said of the advances in organ-transplant techniques. To physicians, for example, the ability to transplant organs has brought the responsibility to do so skill-

More than 100 organ- and tissue-transplant recipients gathered together in 1985 to celebrate National Organ Donor Awareness Week.

fully and wisely. Physicians must now take into consideration which patients are most suitable for organ-transplant surgery and find the best ways to prepare those same patients for surgery and to care for them afterward.

At the same time, organ-transplant success raises new ethical questions that must be answered by all of society. Who should donate organs and who should not? If there are not enough organs for all of those who so desperately need them (and tragically, often there are not), which patients will get those organs? How can we be assured of a better supply of donated organs? Who should pay for organ transplants? And, perhaps most difficult of all, who should decide such questions—moral, legal, and financial—when controversy arises, as it inevitably must?

Like all surgery, organ-transplant surgery still carries risks. All of the obstacles have not yet been overcome, nor are they likely to be in the immediate future. In fact, 100 years from now people may look back on the organ transplantation techniques of the late 20th century as archaic.

But to the patient who receives a new heart or kidney today, such surgery resembles a miracle—one that touches the lives of an ever-increasing number of young people. Some will receive organ transplants or have friends or family members who do. Many will participate in transplants by entering the professions of medicine or scientific research. Most will be able to direct that, should their own life end, their organs be used to give life to someone else. And by exercising their right to vote, they will all help to make laws that determine public policy about transplants—laws that will control how they are treated if they need an organ or wish to donate one.

This book is designed to help young people discover more about organ transplants. It presents the history of this branch of medicine, discusses which organs can be transplanted, and outlines the conditions that make transplants necessary. It considers the problems that occur before and after transplants as well as the various ways in which physicians can solve them. It describes an actual transplant operation and what it is like to have one. Finally, the volume reviews the ways in which law and social policy affect transplants; how research may make the future of organ transplants even more promising than it is today; and how to get more information about organ transplants and becoming an organ donor.

CHAPTER 1

· · · · · · · · · · · · ·

ORGAN TRANSPLANTS THEN AND NOW

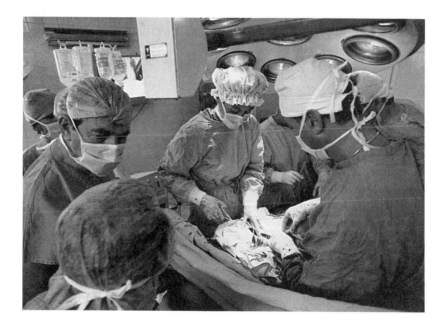

The wish that injured or worn-out body parts might be replaced is an element of the age-old human desire to cure pain and disease, and in doing so, to put off death. In fact, references to transplants have appeared in the religious writings and myths of many cultures since the beginning of recorded time.

In Greek mythology, for example, the Chimera was described as a beast made of parts from many different creatures, including the head of a lion, a goat's body, and a dragon's fiery breath and long, scaly tail. In the 2nd century A.D., according to a Christian story, the saints Cosmas and Damian amputated a patient's leg, then replaced it with the leg of a man who had recently died.

In India, such stories were being translated into reality as early as 300 B.C. In operations that were among the first recorded skin transplants, or grafts, physicians from that era repaired injured noses with pieces of skin from the patients' cheeks or neck.

For hundreds of years, skin grafting was done only by healers in India. But European traders and explorers carried home stories of it, so that by the 16th century A.D. a few Italian healers had become skilled at similar methods. In his book *On the Surgery of Mutilation by Grafting Techniques* the surgeon Gaspare Tagliacozzi described how he rebuilt a patient's nose by carving away scar tissue from the nose area, then cutting a flap of skin partly away from the arm. Molding the flap into a nose shape, he sewed it to the patient's face, but left it partially attached to the arm

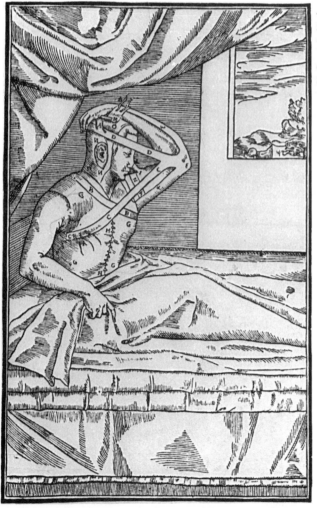

A drawing of the skin-grafting technique used by the surgeon Gaspare Tagliacozzi in the 16th century to rebuild a patient's nose.

from which it had come. Thus the blood supply from the arm kept the flap of skin alive while it healed into place on the face of the patient.

When the skin flap had healed to the face, Tagliacozzi finished cutting it away from the arm and fastened down the new "nose" with a few last stitches. After several more weeks of healing, if all went well, the previously disfigured patient would have a much better-looking face.

In the 16th century, however, there were many factors that worked against the success of a surgical operation. First, anesthesia was unknown at that time. Patients who underwent surgery did so wide-awake, and without medication to deaden the pain.

Next, because no one yet knew that bacteria even existed, surgeons' unclean instruments often carried infections into the surgical wounds. And because there were no antibiotics, patients who got such infections generally died from them.

Finally, the Roman Catholic church—a very powerful force in Italy—did not approve of Tagliacozzi's procedures, which were seen by churchmen as interfering with the "will of God." Such drastic tampering with nature smacked of the devil's work, they thought. Consequently, Tagliacozzi and other surgeons fell into disrepute, and their techniques languished until the 18th century, when the British extended their empire to India. At that time, the ancient Indian grafting procedures were rediscovered by British surgeons.

Among them was John Hunter (1728–93), who was able to graft a patient's knocked-out tooth back into his mouth. A century later, the Swiss surgeon Jaques Reverdin (1842–1928) found that a small piece of a patient's skin, when peeled from a healthy spot and bandaged tightly to a severe wound, would grow larger and help the wound to heal. Around the same time, the Italian Guiseppe Baronio showed that with sheep, large sections of skin could be moved from one place to another on the same animal.

19th-Century Advances

Two very important 19th-century breakthroughs in medical science were in the areas of pain and infection control. In 1846, at the Massachusetts General Hospital in Boston, dentist William T. G. Morton demonstrated the first successful use of general anesthesia by giving ether to a young man and then painlessly removing a tumor from his jaw. In 1877, British surgeon Joseph Lister successfully showed the importance of clean hands and instruments during surgery, and the risk of infection during operations began to decrease.

Encouraged by these advances, 19th-century physicians reported transplanting bone, muscle, and limbs from one person to another, and even from animals into people. But such human-to-human and animal-to-human grafts survived only for very short times—a few weeks at most. The reasons for this were twofold.

First, 19th-century scientific knowledge was not yet advanced enough even to illuminate the true problems of such transplant operations, much less suggest ways to surmount them. Grafting from one human being to another, for example, is much more difficult than simply moving skin from one place to another on a person's body. This is because the body's immune system defends it against living material that is foreign to it. An invasion of harmful bacteria, for example, will activate the immune system, which produces special cells that engulf and destroy the bacteria—thus protecting the body from disease.

But skin from one person transplanted onto the body of another also activates the recipient's immune system, which will destroy the helpful skin graft just as if it were harmful bacteria. The immune system cannot tell the difference between a skin transplant and a bacterial invasion. It only distinguishes between foreign and nonforeign objects—and destroys all those that it recognizes as foreign unless it is stopped from doing so. True animal-to-human grafts are even more difficult to do, and have not been successful over the long-term even in modern times.

The second reason for the failure of most 19th-century surgeons in their transplant attempts was that the very tiny needles and sutures needed for such work had not yet been developed. Fine sewing of blood vessels to one another is necessary to ensure that a transplanted organ receives the blood supply it needs. But it was not until the early 20th century that University of Chicago doctors Alexis Carrel and Charles Guthrie made a breakthrough in the problem of sewing technique in transplant surgery.

Carrel and Guthrie showed that when blood vessels were perfectly sewn together, blood would flow through them just as it had before they were severed. Thus a transplanted organ could

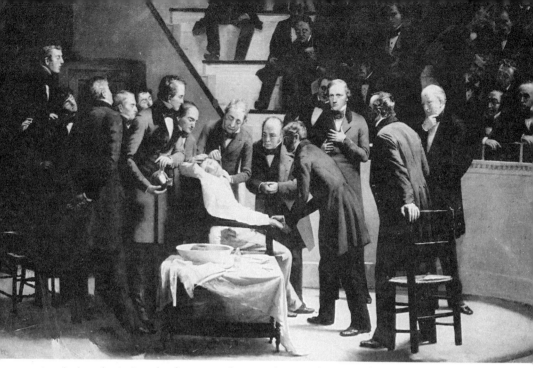

A painting depicting the first use of general anaesthesia at the Massachusetts General Hospital in 1846. During the operation, dentist William T. G. Morton painlessly removed a tumor from a young man's jaw.

be adequately connected to the blood vessels of the person or animal receiving the organ. In one dramatic experiment, Carrel and Guthrie were able to perform a heart transplant on a dog. They also successfully transplanted the kidneys of a cat. These feats showed that such success might also be possible in human beings.

Improved surgical technique, however, could not make up for the most serious obstacle to successful organ transplants—the body's own defenses. Even when the incisions and sutures were done with great precision, and pain and infection were controlled, tissue transplanted from one person to another would often be rejected by the recipient's body.

The Immune System

In the early 1920s, a young Boston surgeon named Emile Holman noticed that if a patient received one set of skin grafts and then later received another, the second set was rejected much faster than the first. It was as if the graft's recipient—the host—had developed antibodies against the skin, just as a person vaccinated against a disease develops antibodies hostile to that disease. (Antibodies, proteins that attack and destroy foreign matter such as disease-causing germs, are the "soldiers" in the immune system's war against harmful invaders.) So Holman theorized that the body rejected foreign tissue through a process much like the one it used to fight off germs—that is, through antibodies.

In the 1940s, a British researcher named Peter Medawar, intent on finding a way to help soldiers and civilians who had been burned during World War II, made groundbreaking discoveries about the tendency of graft recipients to develop antibodies against donated skin. He found that animals exposed to foreign tissue at a very early time in their fetal development would not produce antibodies to that tissue, and so would not reject the same kind of foreign tissue if, later on in life, they received it in a transplant.

Of course, such prebirth exposure was not a practical way to make the bodies of human beings accept transplanted skin or organs. But Medawar's work helped show that the body's rejection of foreign tissue was indeed an immune response. For his pioneering work, Medawar received the Nobel Prize in medicine and physiology in 1960, sharing the prize with Sir Macfarlane Burnet. He is now recognized as the father of modern immunology.

Blood-typing and Early Transplant Attempts

In 1900, the Viennese scientist Karl Landsteiner found that human blood could be categorized into types, and that the human body would reject all blood types that were not its own. This discovery made possible a lifesaving procedure that is really a form of human-to-human transplantation: blood transfusion.

In the early 1950s, when surgeons were ready to attempt human kidney transplants, it was assumed that transplants between persons who had the same type of blood would prove successful in preventing rejection by the recipient's immune system. In 1953, under this assumption, one of the first kidney transplants between humans was done by Dr. David Hume at Peter Brent Brigham Hospital in Boston.

At first it appeared that the procedure had been successful. On the 83rd day after the operation, the patient was allowed to return home. Unfortunately, on the 175th day, he died. Later patients who underwent similar transplantation operations also died. Autopsies showed that despite correct blood-type matching of the kidney donor and recipient, in almost every case the donated kidney had been rejected, causing death. The lesson was clear: Blood-typing was not the whole solution to organ-transplant rejection.

In 1954, however, another surgeon performed a kidney transplant using a kidney donated by the patient's identical twin brother. By 1960, 30 such transplants had been done—all between identical twins—and all of the patients had lived. The reason for this success was that the twins were not only alike in appearance and blood type, but also down to the tiniest elements of their cells (the basic building blocks of the body). The recipient's body did

Dr. Karl Landsteiner was awarded the Nobel Prize for medicine in 1930 for his discovery that human blood may be classified by different types—a process now known as "blood-typing."

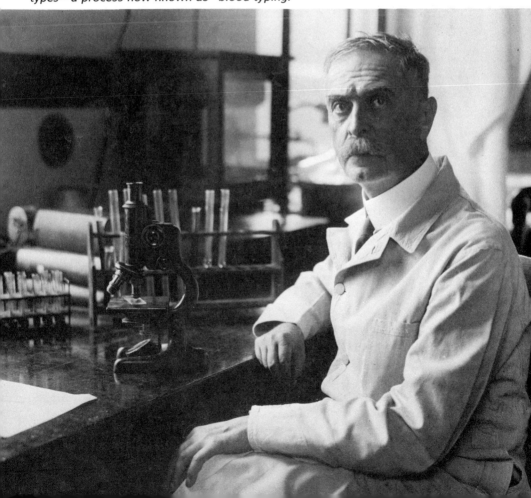

Shown here in 1955, 10 months after receiving one of his twin brother Ronald's kidneys, Richard Herrick (right) was one of the first successful kidney-transplant recipients.

not perceive the donor twin's organ as foreign, and so did not reject it.

Unfortunately, this discovery did not change things for those patients who did not have an identical twin. For these patients, other alternatives were sought. One method that was tried with the hope of preventing rejection was bombarding the organ recipient's whole body with X rays. The radiation succeeded in suppressing the organ recipient's immune response, but it often killed the patient, either by causing *aplastic anemia* (a disease in which the body's ability to make blood cells is destroyed) or by disabling the patient's immune system so completely that the patient died from an infection.

In 1959, Boston physicians Robert Schwarz and William Dameshek made a tremendous breakthrough with their discovery that drugs could suppress the body's immune system and so keep patients from rejecting transplants. Some of the additional and unwanted side-effects of these drugs were potentially just as lethal as those of X rays, and the drugs also disabled both the immune system and the body's ability to make blood cells; but the dosages in which the drugs were given could be adjusted more precisely than X rays, so that patients could survive them.

Tissue Typing and Cyclosporine

In 1960 another major breakthrough was made when Dr. Peter Medawar found a way of typing tissue, just as blood had been typed, allowing organ donors and recipients to be better matched so as to prevent rejection. In 1962, tissue typing and drugs to prevent rejection were successfully used in a human kidney transplant patient.

After that, things happened quickly, because for the first time in history physicians had all the tools necessary for successful human-to-human organ transplants: anesthesia; antibiotics to prevent infections; proper surgical techniques; blood and tissue typing; and immune-suppressing drugs with which to prevent organ rejection.

In 1963, a French surgeon transplanted new bone marrow (the tissue in the center of bones, which makes blood cells) into a young man, curing the man's *leukemia* (a cancer that causes the body to produce malformed blood cells). In the same year Dr. Thomas Starzl of the University of Pittsburgh performed a successful liver transplant. In 1966, a kidney/pancreas transplant was done. And in 1967, South African surgeon Christiaan Barnard performed the first successful heart-transplant surgery on Louis Washkansky.

Throughout the 1970s, work to refine tissue-typing techniques was continued, notably by Dr. Paul I. Terasaki of UCLA, who had begun his scientific career as an assistant to tissue-typing pioneer Peter Medawar. Terasaki was one of several American transplant specialists who traveled to the Soviet Union in 1986 in an attempt to save victims of the Chernobyl nuclear power-plant disaster by giving them bone-marrow transplants to restore their immunity and improve their blood-cell status, which had been severely weakened by exposure to radiation released during the explosion.

In 1972 another breakthrough occurred, this time with the discovery of cyclosporine, a rejection-preventing drug more effective than any of the drugs that had been used before it. After several years of testing, cyclosporine was first used on human organ transplant patients in 1976, with such good results that by 1980 it was being used for almost all types of transplant.

Pittsburgh liver-transplant surgeon Dr. Thomas Starzl called cyclosporine "the key that unlocks the door to transplants." After he began using this drug, the 1-year survival rate of his patients nearly doubled, from 35% to more than 60%. Pioneer heart-transplant surgeon Dr. Norman Shumway of Stanford University remarked that none of his patients had shown symptoms of organ rejection after he began giving them cyclosporine.

Cyclosporine is not a magic potion or surefire miracle drug; it does not prevent rejection or other complications of organ-transplant surgery in every patient. But because of this new drug, said Dr. Bruce Reitz, head of the transplant team at the University of Baltimore, many patients who "were very ill and facing early death" now recover from heart-transplant surgery in as little as four weeks, and others, in as little as eight weeks.

Meanwhile, research on tissue and organ transplantation continues, and optimism for further success with new drugs and surgical techniques is growing. Perhaps at some time in the future, organ donors may become unnecessary; scientists may learn, for example, to create new organs in laboratories by *cloning* (growing whole organs from a single original cell). And as the secrets of the immune system continue to be discovered, simpler and safer ways of preventing organ rejection may also be learned. For the present, we can remain hopeful, understanding that recent successes are spurring even more investigation of transplantation. "It will take a number of (additional) breakthroughs," said Dr. Charles Baxter, medical director of Transplant Services at the University of Texas, "but I think in the next decade we will find a lot of new approaches that will advance transplants even more dramatically."

•   •   •   •

. . . .

CHAPTER 2

WHICH ORGANS —AND WHY?

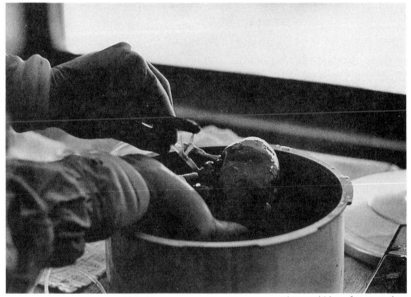

A human kidney for transplant

All organ transplantation takes tremendous skill on the part of surgeons and other health-care professionals, and almost all transplants have lifelong side effects. People who undergo organ transplants need to have frequent medical checkups afterward, and most must take immune-suppressing medication for the rest of their life. Some kinds of transplant still carry considerable risk, and some organs cannot yet be successfully transplanted from one person to another.

But many types of transplant have become almost routine, and are considered so safe as to be regularly performed, not only to prevent death, but to improve the quality of life as well. For a patient who might otherwise remain bedridden, hooked up to a dialysis machine (see page 67) on a regular basis, or restricted by physical disability to living the life of an invalid, organ transplants offer a new hope of leading a relatively normal and active life.

Cornea Transplants and Lens Implants

Two types of eye-transplantation surgery fall into the category of being almost routine: corneal-transplant surgery and artificial-lens implantation. The cornea is a thin transparent membrane in the front part of the eyeball. Like the crystal of a watch, it protects the inner tissue of the eye. If the cornea is scarred or clouded by injury or infection so that it is no longer clear, blindness in the afflicted eye may result. To restore sight, surgeons snip out a circular area of the damaged cornea, and replace it with a section of cornea from a donated eye.

The donor eye is obtained from a specialized organ bank called an eye bank. Organ banks are used to store organs (those which

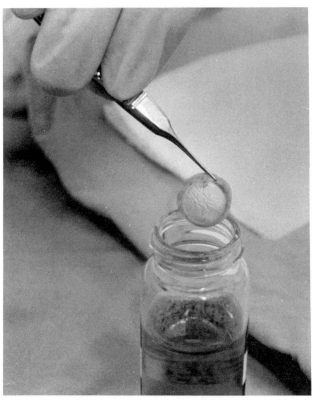

A human cornea for transplant is placed in a preservative fluid. Cornea transplants were the first transplants to be regularly performed and are now successful in restoring sight to more than 90% of the recipients.

can be stored) that people have donated for transplantation at the time of their death. Transplantation operations that use an organ from a donor who is not the twin of the recipient—which is almost always the case with transplants from an organ bank—are called *allografts*: literally, "other grafts." Eye banks have been in existence since the 1940s, and cornea transplants were among the first and most successful of all transplants.

Corneal transplants can be done under local anesthesia—with painkilling eyedrops or an injection of a painkilling drug into the tissue near the eye—or under general anesthesia, where the patient is unconscious during the operation. They are successful more than 90% of the time, because unlike most other body tissues, the cornea has no direct blood supply. Thus the body's rejection mechanisms—most of which are carried by the blood—cannot reach and reject the transplanted cornea.

The lens is another transparent portion of the eye that may be damaged by injury or disease. Just as moving a camera lens focuses a camera, movement of the lens in the eye focuses vision and allows us to see both near and distant objects. Its attachment within the eye is too complex for transplantation of the lens itself, but this delicate organ can be replaced with a clear acrylic substitute. Although the artificial lens cannot move as the natural one would, and the patient must wear glasses to see objects nearby, such implants do restore clear distant vision.

Bone Transplants

Because bone is another type of tissue that is not in direct contact with the blood, it too may readily be transplanted from one person to another. As early as 1890, the Scottish surgeon W. Macewen had discovered this. He removed part of a child's diseased arm bone and replaced it with wedges of bone removed during surgical operations on six other patients. Macewen's graft grew so perfectly that when the child reached adulthood, his diseased arm was only seven centimeters shorter than his unaffected arm, and he earned a living by doing heavy labor.

In modern times, one common reason for bone-transplant surgery is nonunion of a fracture, in which a gap is left between the parts of a broken bone. It may also be done after a cancerous tumor of the bone has been removed. Today, surgeons immobilize the bone in such cases by linking together the remaining

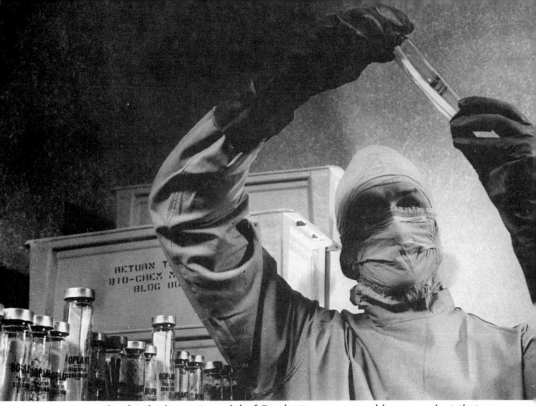

A scientist inspects a vial of Boplant, a processed bone product that can be used for transplant in place of donated human bone.

sections with a metal nail, then packing the gap of missing bone with donated bone chips. The chips form a kind of scaffolding over which the body will regenerate its own bone tissue.

Bone for transplantation may be obtained from various locations in the patient's body—a transplant that is called an *autograft* (a to-myself transplant)—or it may be bone that is donated and stored in a bone bank until needed. At some transplant centers, the success rate for bone transplants is as high as 80%.

The other human organs that can be transplanted are unlike bone or the cornea and lens of the eye in that they are directly supplied by blood vessels and so are more susceptible to rejection by the body. When these organs are transplanted as allografts, the body's tendency to reject them must be overcome.

Skin Grafts

Skin is among the most difficult of organs to transplant from one person to another; in most cases, allografts of skin cannot be done at all. But some method of replacing skin is often desperately needed, for skin—the body's barrier between itself and a hostile environment—is frequently damaged by burn injuries. Currently, autografting—taking skin from an uninjured part of the patient's body and grafting it over the injured part—is the only successful method of skin grafting.

Autografted skin transplants may be *flap grafts*, in which the transplanted skin is not completely severed from the donor site (the place it is taken from) until it has developed a good blood supply at the recipient site (the place to which it is transplanted). The procedure for creating flap grafts is complicated and uncomfortable, but its results are good: The success rate for these grafts is very high, and the procedure may cure what would otherwise have been a disfiguring scar or deformity.

Full-thickness autografts involve moving small pieces of whole skin—all the skin's layers—from one place on the body to another. They are especially useful on the face, where minimum scarring is an important objective after injuries or disfiguring

An 11-year-old burn victim is comforted by a friend. Skin grafting can improve the appearance of many burn victims, who otherwise would be left with disfiguring scars.

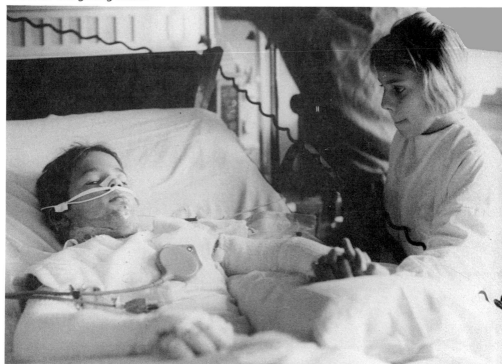

diseases. But because full-thickness grafts do not have a blood supply while they heal, they do not succeed quite as often as flap grafts.

Split-thickness autografts involve moving layers of skin as thin as tissue paper from one body site to another. They heal well, and because they are so thin, large numbers of them may be harvested from undamaged areas of the patient's body. Once healed, however, split-thickness grafts tend to have a shiny reddish appearance, which makes them less than ideal for grafting to exposed areas such as the face.

Donated human skin, or skin from other species (such as pigs), is sometimes used to cover very large and serious burns. Such grafts are not expected to take; instead, they are used to prevent the patient's body from losing critical amounts of fluid through the burned area, and to protect it from infection. This is necessary because burn patients are sometimes too critically ill to undergo autograft surgery, or because their burns cover so much of their body that they have little uninjured skin to use for transplantation.

If the body did not reject foreign skin so aggressively, donated human skin could be transplanted to severely burned patients. But at present, the rejection of donated skin is a problem that has not been solved satisfactorily. In an effort to get around this difficulty, a team of researchers at the Massachusetts Institute of Technology, led by plastic surgeons Dr. John Burke and Ioannis Yannis, Ph.D., is working on the development of an artificial skin that is not rejected by the human body. Made from cowhide, shark cartilage, and plastic, the skin is called *glycosaminoglycan*, and studies of its use on approximately 80 severely burned patients are now under way.

Another approach to solving the problem of skin rejection is being taken by Dr. Eugene Bell, a former Massachusetts Institute of Technology professor. In 1986, Dr. Bell founded a company called Organogenesis, which is attempting, among other things, to grow, from only a few original, donated cells, real human skin and other whole organs that human bodies will not reject. While the general use of such laboratory-grown skin and organs may be years away, Dr. Bell is confident that he will eventually be able to grow not just skin, but entire thyroid glands, pancreases, and blood vessels for transplanting into patients who need them.

Blood-Vessel Transplants

Blood-vessel transplantation is a frequently needed procedure; *peripheral vascular disease*, in which blood vessels become obstructed by deposits containing fatty and fibrous material (hardening of the arteries), is one of the most common and serious diseases of the legs. This disease can also block vessels that nourish the heart, which can lead to a heart attack. At present, surgeons can bypass such obstructed areas of a blood vessel by taking a nonessential vein from the patient's leg and using it to route blood around the blocked area. But for people whose nonessential vessels are in poor condition and who have no vessels that can be moved to essential areas, surgeons must use synthetic vessels made of Dacron or Teflon. These artificial materials work because they are smooth, thus preventing blood from clotting on their inner surfaces and forming blockages. They also do not trigger the body's immune response, and are therefore not rejected by it.

Bone-Marrow Transplants

Bone marrow—the tissue in the center of bones that produces blood cells—is yet another type of tissue that is difficult to transplant. As noted in Chapter 1, leukemia is one disease that can be treated with transplanted bone marrow. But because all of a patient's bone marrow is often affected by diseases such as leukemia, autografting of marrow can be done only if the patient's disease goes into remission—that is, if the disease becomes temporarily inactive. During a period of remission, the patient's own bone marrow may be removed through a long, hollow needle, in a procedure called *bone marrow aspiration*. The healthy marrow removed by this method is stored so that later, when the disease flares up again, the marrow can be grafted back into the patient's body.

If the patient has an identical twin, or a relative whose tissue type is very similar to his or her own, donated marrow may be allografted. (Transplants between identical twins are classified as autografts, because the tissues involved are identical.)

One particularly dreaded complication of bone-marrow transplantation is graft-versus-host disease, a reversal of the usual rejection reaction. In it, the transplanted tissue reacts against the

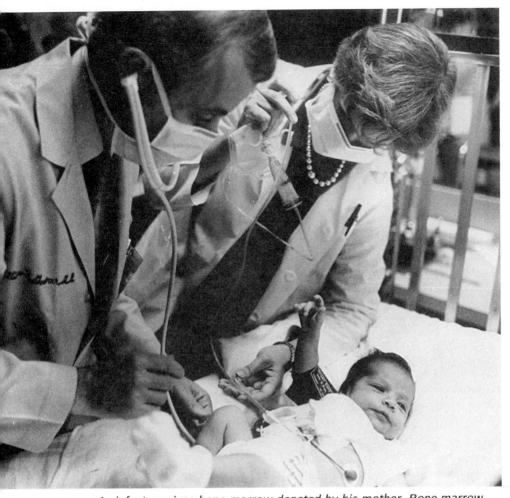

An infant receives bone marrow donated by his mother. Bone-marrow transplants between identical twins or family members with similar tissue type are considered to be the most successful.

host's body, instead of the body reacting against the transplanted tissue. Once a graft-versus-host reaction has begun, it is difficult to control, and often proves fatal to the patient. In general, the success of bone-marrow transplantation depends partly upon the type of disease being treated, and averages about 50%.

Many organs of the body can be more easily allografted than skin, blood vessels, and bone marrow. This is because cyclosporine and other drugs can suppress the body's natural tendency to reject many of these allografts. Among the organs that can be allografted are the kidney, the liver, and the heart.

Kidney Transplants

One of the kidney's major functions is to process waste products from the body. Without it, the body would be poisoned by waste products resulting from its metabolism, the process by which the body converts food to energy.

Patients whose kidneys function poorly or not at all may have these waste products removed for a while by a process called *dialysis*. In this process, waste materials are artificially removed by passing the blood through a filtering membrane in a dialysis machine. The cleansed blood is then returned to the body. (In another type of dialysis, called peritoneal dialysis, cleansing fluid is put into the patient's abdominal cavity through a tube. Peritoneal dialysis can also be used for cleansing waste products from persons with kidney disease.)

Dialysis is not as perfect as the body's natural way of removing waste; besides being tiring and time-consuming, dialysis also requires the patient to stay on a very restricted diet. Chronic kidney dialysis is so burdensome, in fact, that patients undergoing it often want kidney transplants even though these have a lower long-term success rate than dialysis. Nonetheless, such patients may now often have their wish granted because—largely thanks to cyclosporine—kidney transplantation has become one of the biggest success stories in organ transplantation. Between 1954 and 1973 only about 10,000 kidney transplants were performed. But in 1986 alone, nearly 9,000 such operations were done, up from 5,300 just 4 years earlier.

The popular young television actor Gary Coleman is one of the many people who have undergone successful kidney transplants. The success rate for this type of transplantation is now approaching 90%, and a patient whose body rejects the new kidney can return to dialysis and await a second, or even third or fourth, kidney transplant.

Liver Transplants

The liver is another organ that can now be transplanted, although transplantation of the liver is more complex and risky than kidney transplantation. The liver is the body's largest organ. Located under the lower ribs, it occupies all of the upper right side of the abdomen and part of the left side as well. The liver has two main functions: It produces chemicals that are vital to the body, and it neutralizes poisons and wastes that are deadly to it. These functions are absolutely necessary to life.

The liver may fail because of inborn or *congenital* abnormalities, infection, cancerous tumors, or other ailments including damage caused by excessive drinking. In many of these cases, a liver transplant must be performed in order to save the patient's life.

Removal of the diseased liver is in itself dangerous, because the patient is usually ill when such surgery is undertaken. If the donated liver does not work at once, the patient will die because there is no artificial support system for the liver, as there is with kidney dialysis for kidney-failure patients.

Still, several hundred livers have been successfully transplanted, and several liver recipients are still alive more than two years after receiving their transplants. In 1986, there were more than 900 liver-transplantation attempts, up from only 62 in 1982, and the success rate for this surgical operation is now about 70% in terms of patients and grafts surviving for a year after transplantation.

Heart and Lung Transplants

Among the most dramatic organ transplants are those involving the heart and lungs. The heart is the body's blood pump; the lungs are its oxygen pumps. Together these organs form a system as important in human myth, folklore, and imagination as it is in the body itself, for even in ancient times the heart was known as the very seat of life.

The heart may fail because of *myopathy* (muscle weakness) resulting from infection or from unknown causes or because of congenital defects. Because the heart pumps blood directly to the lungs, heart failure may cause the lungs to fail as well. Patients who need heart or heart-lung transplants are usually confined to bed, too weak to move and in some cases too weak even to breathe without mechanical respirators. Until very recently, little could be done for such unfortunate people; they simply grew weaker until they finally died.

But the years between 1982 and 1986 have seen tremendous growth in the number of heart and heart-lung transplants. And over the same time, the success rates for these transplants have improved dramatically. In 1986, more than 1,300 heart trans-

Liver-transplant recipient Joshua Kelley relaxes in his mother's arms. Liver transplants are especially risky, because if the donated liver does not begin to function immediately the patient will die.

plants were performed, and 45 heart-lung transplants were done, compared with only 7 in 1982. (Because the blood vessels of the heart and lung are so interrelated, these two organs are usually transplanted together even when the patient really needs only the lung. This is primarily because the survival rate for heart-lung transplants is better than that for lung transplants alone.)

The 1-year success rate for heart transplants is now about 85%, and for heart-lung transplants, about 50%. Increased technical skill among surgeons is responsible for some of the improvement of the success rates of organ transplantation. But other technical improvements have also come a long way since the first organ transplants were performed. Today, sophisticated new procedures allow doctors to match organs with recipients so that rejection is minimalized and the patient receives the organ most closely matched to his or her own tissue.

In the next chapter we will discuss how this cross matching takes place, what criteria it is based on, and the factors the physician must take into account before approving a person for organ-transplant surgery.

•   •   •   •

CHAPTER 3

· · · · · · · · · · · · · ·

THE PERFECT MATCH

The United Network for Organ Sharing

Not every person who wishes to receive an organ transplant is an ideal candidate for one. Because of this, it is up to physicians to decide which patients are best suited to transplantation. The American Medical Association has issued the following guidelines to aid physicians in making this decision.

First, a person who is to receive an organ transplant should have given informed consent. This means that a potential transplant recipient should understand the operation that is to be done, the positive effects it may have, and also what might possibly go wrong during the surgery and with the transplanted organ. The patient then must freely agree to take the risks of surgery in order to reap the possible benefits.

Second, the risks of surgery required for transplanting an organ should be in proportion to the possible benefits; one would not do heart-transplant surgery, for example, to cure a minor heart condition that can be controlled by drugs. Furthermore, the patient should be ill enough to warrant the transplant operation, but not too ill to survive it.

Third, the patient should have no other serious complicating disease, and should not have any infections. Thus, for example, a patient whose kidneys have failed but who is also dying of lung cancer would not be a candidate for a kidney transplant, because he or she could not substantially benefit from it. Patients with infections also cannot receive transplants until the infections have been cleared up, because the immune-suppressing drugs they receive after transplantation surgery will allow the infections to flourish and even kill them.

Fourth, a patient's age may be considered in deciding whether or not to perform a transplantation operation. In general, younger patients are favored, not only because they can better withstand the surgery, but also because a young person will be able to enjoy the benefits of a transplant for more years than an older one. This, however, is not a hard-and-fast rule; it often depends upon the individual circumstances involved.

Fifth, most surgeons seek evidence of mental and emotional health in transplant candidates. A good mental outlook is an important factor in successful recovery, because people who strongly desire and expect to get well are more apt to do the things that are necessary for recovery: to get up and walk as soon as medically possible, for example, even though it may cause them pain to do so. Also, for the transplant to succeed over time, a patient must be mentally healthy enough to accurately describe his or her symptoms after the transplant has been made, take medication reliably, control his or her diet, and avoid organ-damaging habits such as illicit drug use, smoking, and excessive drinking.

Once it has been decided that a patient is a suitable candidate for transplant surgery, an organ compatible with the patient must be found. Which organ, from among the limited number of donated organs that are available, will be best for this patient to receive?

Who Receives a Donated Organ?

The decisions that must be made about who will receive a particular organ and who must continue to wait to receive one are based on solid medical criteria. The hospital that has the responsibility of removing a donated organ notifies a local or national organization that has a computerized system that matches organs and their possible recipients. All pertinent information about the organ is fed into this computerized system, which in turn prints out a list of well-matched recipient candidates in order of their suitability.

A number of factors determine the suitability of a candidate to receive an organ. The first and most obvious requirement is that the available organ be of the right size needed to perform its vital function in the recipient's body, and at the same time, not be too large to fit into the cavity that will be left when the nonfunctioning organ is removed. A grown man's kidney, for example, will not fit into an infant's abdomen; and a tiny heart, no matter how well transplanted, will not pump enough blood to keep a grown man alive.

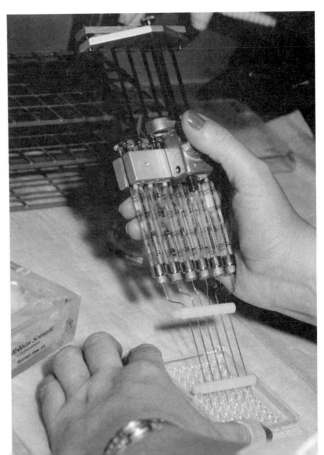

Tissue typing, shown being done here, allows doctors to make the best match possible between donor and recipient.

Next, the recipient's blood type should be the same as that of the organ donor, and the tissue type of the donor and recipient should be as similar as possible, in order to minimize the recipient's rejection reaction against the newly transplanted organ. Although we now know that it is possible to use drugs to control the body's immune-defense mechanisms against foreign tissue, it is better to avoid rejection reactions as much as possible. This minimizes the required dosages of immune-suppressing drugs, and thus their potential side effects.

The tissue typing that is done on an organ and its prospective recipient to see whether they are matched to one another is performed in a laboratory. A technician mixes white blood cells

Ruth Foisy (right) donated her kidney to Alicia Sferrino, the daughter she gave up for adoption 20 years before.

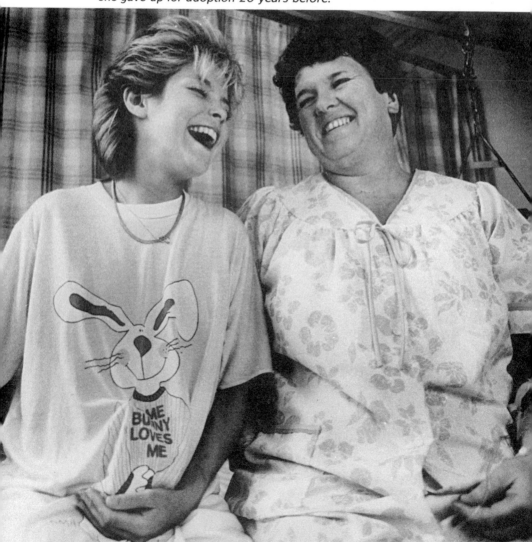

called *leukocytes* from both the donated organ and the potential organ recipient with serum (the clear fluid that remains when red blood cells are removed from blood) that has already been typed. If this *typing serum* kills similar numbers of leukocytes from both the organ donor and the organ recipient, the technician knows that the donor organ and potential recipient have at least some of the immune-rejection-provoking substance known as *human leukocyte antigens* (HL-A) in common. HL-A are proteins on the surface of white blood cells. Of the 75 types that have been identified, each person is born with 8—4 from their father and 4 from their mother. In tissue typing, the more alike the tissue reactions from both donor and recipient, the more successful the transplant operation is likely to be.

Patients accepted for transplant surgery are tissue typed at once, and the results are entered into the nationwide network described earlier. Organs that become available for donation are also tissue typed, and this vital information is fed into the same computer system, where it becomes one of the primary factors in deciding organ compatibility.

Because there are at least 32 different human leukocyte antigens, it is extremely unlikely that 2 unrelated persons will be identical with respect to all of these antigens, and therefore be of identical tissue type. Thus, a reasonably workable similarity of tissue type is usually the best that can be hoped for. If, however, a patient is so ill that he or she will die unless a transplantation is done at once, surgeons may perform the operation using an organ that is not as closely tissue matched to the recipient as possible. This means that the surgeons must prescribe larger doses of immune-suppressing drugs for the patient in an attempt to overcome the difference in tissue type. In most cases, however, if a transplant is not needed urgently, surgeons will wait for a well-matched organ to become available.

The best organs for transplantation are live organs—those that have been removed from a living donor. In the case of most organs for transplantation, living donations are not possible, because the organs that could be donated are needed to sustain life in human beings. In the case of kidney transplants, however, living donations are possible because each human being has two kidneys, and only one is really necessary for the body to function properly. Bone marrow may also be transplanted from a living donor. Almost all live donations are performed between family members.

The other type of organs available for transplantation are called cadaver organs, because they are removed from the body of a person who has just died or whose brain is dead but whose heart has continued to beat, often with help from life-sustaining machines. If the heart, which supplies blood to all vital organs, can be kept pumping in a person who has no chance of recovery, then the organs of that person can be preserved for a few hours until they can be removed for transplantation.

Organs cannot be removed from a donor's body until he or she has been declared brain dead by a team of surgeons who are not in any way involved with removing or transplanting the organs. Even after a person is declared brain dead, and even if that person signed an organ-donor card, the donor's family must give their approval before the organs may be removed for transplantation.

In most of the United States today, the law requires that some member of the hospital staff approach the family of the deceased and ask whether or not it is their wish that his or her organs be donated. In even greater numbers of hospitals across the United States, the person responsible for asking this delicate question is the organ-transplant coordinator. This person must not only speak with the family of the deceased, but also make arrangements for the removal of his or her organs, initiate a search for a suitable recipient, and make arrangements for the transport of the organs to the recipient.

Once removed from the donor's body, cadaver organs are at once chilled in order to slow their deterioration. They can be kept only for a short time before they deteriorate so badly that they are useless for transplantation. Kidneys can be preserved for up to 72 hours, livers up to 12 hours, hearts for up to 4 hours, and heart-lungs for only 1 to 2 hours. The exception to this rule is the cornea, which does not receive a direct blood supply and can be removed as long as 12 hours after death and kept for a longer period.

Organs for transplantation must also be free of disease and infection. It would make little sense to give a patient a kidney that does not function well because it is scarred from earlier disease, for example, or a liver that has been damaged by the donor's excessive alcohol or drug use. Furthermore, an infected organ that had been subjected to immune-system-suppressant drugs would be destroyed by uncontrollable infection.

All of these requirements unavoidably limit the number of suitable organs available to any given patient—as does the fact that the supply of donor organs is always smaller than the demand for them.

In 1986, for example, more than 8,000 kidneys were transplanted— but 10,000 more patients waited in vain for kidney transplants because donor organs were not available. More than 900 liver transplants were also performed in 1986, but no livers could be found for 300 more patients who needed them. There were more than 1,300 heart transplants done in 1986, but 450 more would have been performed had suitable donated hearts been available. And 45 heart-lung transplants were done, but 91 more patients could not have this potentially lifesaving surgery because no suitable donor organs were available.

Transplant coordinator Mary Jean McAleer listens for news of a possible heart donor. Transplant coordinators not only initiate the search for organs needed for transplant but are also responsible for approaching the family members of deceased patients, in an effort to procure organs.

In order to improve this situation, the United States government has enacted a law contained within the Omnibus Budget Act of 1986. Under the law, all hospitals in which organ transplants are performed will have to be members of an already existing national organ-sharing network: the United Network for Organ Sharing (UNOS), based in Richmond, Virginia.

A nonprofit group partly supported by federal funds, UNOS has a computer system that lists patients needing transplants and helps locate the best recipient for each donated organ. In 1987, the network had 244 members, including 164 hospitals, 19 laboratories, and 14 public-service agencies that helped to procure organs for donation.

Under the new law, hospitals must join UNOS in order to receive Medicare or Medicaid funds (money that pays for health care to the poor and elderly). And because 97% of the nation's hospitals receive such funds and wish to continue to do so, most are expected to cooperate with UNOS. Thus it is hoped that in the future, many more donated organs will be available to patients who need them.

•　　　　•　　　　•　　　　•

CHAPTER 4

. . . .

THE BODY VIGILANT

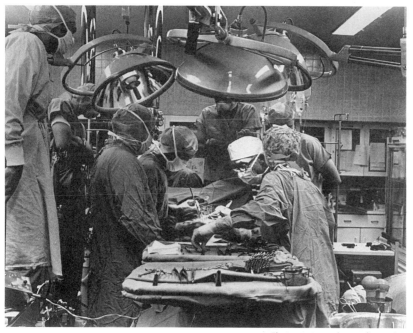

First surgery using cyclosporine

Once a donated organ has been transplanted into a host's body, one of the main obstacles to its survival is rejection by the host. Organ-transplant rejection is caused by the immune system—the human body's system of self-defense.

The immune system combats disease-causing germs, allowing the body to resist infection; without the immune system, even a slight infection could cause death. The virus that causes cold sores, for instance, *herpes simplex*, may spread fatally throughout the body of an immune-suppressed person. Even *Escherichia coli*, a species of bacteria normally present in the human intestine, may become deadly to a patient whose immune system is suppressed.

The elements of the body's immune system are carried mainly in the blood, where special cells called *lymphocytes* circulate. When these cells identify foreign chemical structures called *antigens* on the surface of invading cells such as bacteria, they produce complex proteins known as *antibodies* to destroy the antigen-carrying invaders. But lymphocytes cannot tell the difference between a harmful invader such as a disease-causing germ and a helpful one such as a transplanted organ. Because of this, the immune system often attacks organs that have been transplanted into the body, just as it attacks harmful invaders.

After undergoing transplant surgery, patients are watched vigilantly for symptoms of transplant rejection. These symptoms include fever, swelling, high blood pressure, an aching like that which accompanies influenza, and abnormal blood-test results. The transplanted organ itself may be monitored by a method called tissue biopsy. In tissue biopsy, a small bit of the organ is removed from the host's body through a long, hollow needle. The cells in this small piece of organ are then examined under a microscope to check for early signs of rejection that can be detected before the patient feels the symptoms of such rejection. In this way, rejection can be discovered and treated as soon and as effectively as possible.

Until the early 1980s, the medical methods for combating transplant rejection were uncomfortable and dangerous for patients. Large doses of steroids (substances similar to the hormones produced by the body) lessened the rejection reaction but caused such serious side effects as high blood pressure, ulcers, bleeding, and diabetes (a disease in which the body is unable to process sugar).

Treatment with radiation and harsh drugs such as nitrogen mustard and 6-mercaptopurine, which prevent the normal development of all lymphocytes, was also used to suppress the immune system. Patients receiving these treatments were made helpless in fighting off infection, and in some cases their bone marrow stopped producing new blood cells. These patients often died from pneumonia or other diseases caused by infection, or from a critical lack of blood cells (aplastic anemia).

Overcoming the Rejection Obstacle

Today, rejection is still a serious problem in organ-transplant surgery, but the use of cyclosporine is a powerful new means of fighting against this phenomenon. The story of cyclosporine began in 1972, when a group of scientists at Sandoz Pharmaceuticals, a Swiss drug company, were investigating a fungus imported from Norway. They found that this fungus produced an unusual substance, called cyclosporine, that suppressed the immune system in a way no one had seen before.

Most immune-suppressing drugs then known had the effect of almost completely shutting down the immune system of patients to whom they were given. But cyclosporine left much of this vital system intact, because it curbed only one part of the immune system—a special kind of lymphocyte called a T-helper cell. (The T-helper is one kind of cell that signals other lymphocytes to attack invading cells.)

One scientist at Sandoz, Jean Borel, was especially curious about the new substance, but the company's managers were not interested in developing cyclosporine. The market for the drug was small, they said, and producing it in quantity would be tremendously expensive. For a time, it looked as if research on cyclosporine would be abandoned. Borel, however, was stubborn; he persuaded Sandoz to let him continue studying cyclosporine.

In 1976, Borel told transplant surgeon R. Y. Calne and scientist David White—of England's Cambridge University—about cyclosporine. Intrigued, White and Calne gave the drug to animals that had undergone experimental organ transplants. They found that cyclosporine prevented transplant rejection in the animals, and suggested that it might do the same in human beings. Therefore, in 1978, Sandoz researchers tested the drug on human volunteers to make sure it would not have serious side effects and to learn the proper dosage in which to give it to humans.

Now came an unexpected obstacle: Cyclosporine had to be taken by mouth, but in humans who took it in this way it passed through the digestive system without being absorbed. And unabsorbed, it was useless. Seeing the results of the tests of cyclosporine on human volunteers, Borel wondered whether all his work had been useless, too. But then it occurred to him that

Immune System Rejection of a Transplant

The immune system perceives the tissues of its own body as self. It does that by recognizing identification tags, or markers, on all the cells in the body it has known since shortly after conception. Whenever the immune system meets with any kind of cell or other material in the body, it checks the identification tags to determine if it is self and, therefore, belongs there, or if it is nonself and must be driven from the body. This is the normal and ongoing work the immune system performs to protect the body from invasion by bacteria, viruses, and cancer cells, among other things.

When a transplant has been performed, the immune system perceives the new tissue as nonself because it has someone else's identification tag and therefore attempts to rid the body of the foreign invader. It does this by exploring the transplanted organ with cells called helper lympho-cytes, which have receptors (eyes with which to see and hands with which to hold). When the helper lymphocytes discover nonself material in the body, they release biochemical signals to call other cells into action. When the other cells arrive, they are instructed by the helpers to kill the foreign invader. These new cells are called killer lymphocytes. In order for the killers to know how to find the foreign invaders, the helper cells assist the killer cells to produce receptors that can see and hold onto the transplanted cells. The killers find the transplanted cells and hold onto them tightly as they inject a toxin that kills the transplanted cells. When the transplanted cells are killed, the transplant has been rejected by the body.

Dr. Sandra L. Nehlsen-Cannarella
Director, Immunology Center,
Loma Linda University
Medical Center

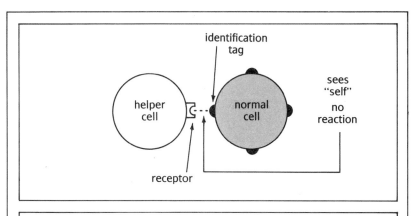

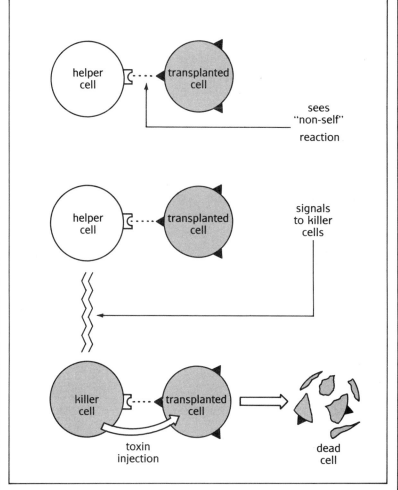

when tested in humans, the drug had been put into gelatin capsules, and the volunteers had swallowed the capsules with water. Perhaps it had not been cyclosporine itself but the method of giving it that had been at fault.

To test his theory, Borel mixed cyclosporine in alcohol, added a chemical to help it dissolve, and swallowed the mixture himself. Afterward, cyclosporine was found to be present in his blood, proving that his body had absorbed it.

By 1980, the Food and Drug Administration had approved cyclosporine for experimental use in organ-transplant patients in a few medical centers around the United States. Almost at once, the remarkable worth of the drug was recognized.

In 1979, Dr. Norman Shumway, the pioneering Stanford University heart-transplant surgeon, was able to keep only 63% of his heart-transplant patients alive for at least a year. But after a year of giving cyclosporine to his patients, the rate at which they survived for a year jumped to 83%. Results in liver transplants were similarly encouraging, with the 1-year survival rate doubling from about 35% to nearly 70%. It was also found that

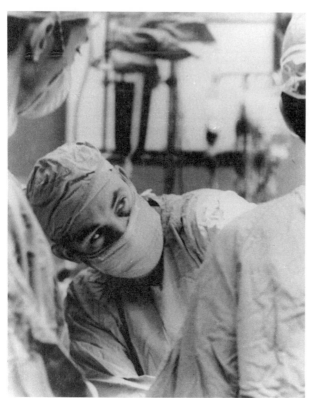

Pioneer heart-transplant surgeon Dr. Norman Shumway watched the 1-year survival rate of his heart-transplant patients climb from 63% to 83% just a year after the introduction of cyclosporine.

patients who had received cyclosporine recovered from transplant surgery more quickly and enjoyed better ongoing health than those who did not receive it.

According to a recent report by Dr. David Winter, director of Medical Research for Sandoz Pharmaceuticals, the 1-year-survival rate for kidney-transplant patients has risen from 83% to more than 90% since cyclosporine was first approved for general use in 1983. And 85% of heart-transplant patients now survive for more than a year after surgery, compared with 59% before cyclosporine was available.

Currently marketed by Sandoz Pharmaceuticals under the brand-name Sandimmune, cyclosporine does not prevent rejection in every single transplant recipient and it does have unpleasant as well as potentially life-threatening side effects. It has been known to cause lymphoma (cancer of the immune system) and sometimes causes abnormal functioning of the kidneys or liver, as well as excess facial hair growth, mouth sores, and an increased sensitivity to heat and cold.

The side effects of cyclosporine are pronounced and widespread throughout the body because the cells it affects—T-lymphocytes—are crucial to the body's proper functioning and are present almost everywhere in the body. One of the drugs often given along with cyclosporine, prednisone, also has side effects, including facial swelling, weight gain, increased quantities of sugar in the blood, and bone brittleness.

Immune-suppressing drugs are also expensive. Cyclosporine is measured in cubic centimeters (cc), and one cc costs about $3.40. Because a daily dose might be 10 cc (the required dose depends on the patient's weight), the cost of cyclosporine could be as high as $34.00 per day, or more than $12,000 per year, and this does not include other drugs and treatments the transplant recipient needs. And as far as researchers know, organ-transplant recipients must take immune-suppressing drugs for the rest of their life.

A Second Chance

Even if a recipient's body does reject a transplanted organ, the recipient does not have to give up hope of successfully receiving a transplanted organ. Some patients have had three or more kidney transplant operations. Patients whose transplanted heart is rejected may also undergo at least one additional transplant attempt. Depending upon the organ involved, the failing transplant can sometimes function long enough to permit a search for a new organ; sometimes mechanical assistance such as kidney dialysis or the use of an artificial heart can bridge the gap between the time when a transplanted organ fails and a new one is found.

Unfortunately, the possibility of a second transplant if a first fails is not available to all transplant patients. Patients who undergo heart-lung transplants, for example, are often too ill to survive a second operation, even if a new set of organs can quickly be found for them. And there is no practical mechanical substitute for the lungs as there is for the kidney and, to a lesser degree, for the heart. Patients in whom a liver transplant fails often do not survive either. Again, this is because a liver transplant often has very severe side effects, and there is not yet any artificial substitute for the liver.

Naturally, it would be ideal if a new drug could be found that completely prevented rejection from occurring. Unfortunately, no such drug appears on the immediate horizon. However, researchers have identified several promising new substances for preventing rejection. Among them is an improved cyclosporine that has fewer undesirable side-effects.

Meanwhile, investigation of the body's immune system is under way in numerous research centers throughout the world, primarily with the hope of discovering ways to combat acquired immune deficiency syndrome (AIDS), a deadly disease that breaks down the body's immune system.

But a better understanding of the immune system will not only help patients with immune deficiencies; improved knowledge of the body's defense systems will benefit all kinds of people—including transplant patients—for whom better control of the immune system is a vital key to longer and healthier survival.

•   •   •   •

How A Heart Transplant Happens

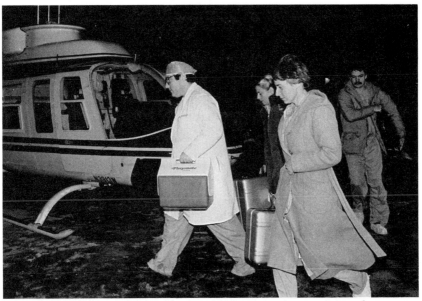

A surgeon carrying a donated heart arrives at an airport. Hearts for transplant must be transported immediately after their removal, in a cooler filled with plasma.

Heart transplants may provide patients who are suffering from serious heart failure with a new chance to lead a relatively normal, healthy life. It may also be the only option open to patients with inoperable heart damage. In order to be put on the waiting list for a new heart, patients must first undergo a variety of tests to determine whether they are physically and emotionally stable enough to be a candidate for transplant. Some of these tests determine whether the patient is suffering from blood clots or infections. Blood clots can render the transplanted heart totally useless, and in transplant patients, who must take enormous doses of immunosuppressant drugs, infections can run rampant and prove fatal. The patient's mental health is also tested because much of the success of

Surgeons must scrub thoroughly before performing organ transplant surgery. Germs and infection are especially deadly to transplant patients because of all the immunosuppressant drugs they must take.

transplant surgery depends on the motivation to survive within each patient.

Family support is also essential, and in many programs it is a mandatory requirement. The family of the transplant patient must understand and fully accept the emotional and financial responsibilities a heart transplant involves. For example, many transplant programs require that the potential candidate live within commuting distance of the hospital, which often makes it necessary for the family to take up at least temporary residence near the hospital. Often such families rent apart-ments or motel rooms; in any case, the cost is very high and must be borne by the family alone.

Once the patient is accepted into the transplant program, he or she is tissue typed and the results are fed into a national computer system that matches donors and recipients. The patient is placed on a waiting list based on need and availability, and the waiting begins. While waiting for an organ, the patient must visit the hospital on a regular, often weekly, basis to have his or her condition evaluated. Patients who develop blood clots, infections, or other serious complications at this point are removed from the list until the problem clears up.

Once a heart becomes available for transplant, the chosen recipient is notified and asked to go to the hospital where the transplant is to take place. There the candidate will be tested once again to see if he or she is fit to undergo surgery. The person is then prepared the way all other surgical patients are: He or she is cleansed to prevent infections and is not allowed to eat or drink the night before the operation in order to prevent food from backing up into the windpipe or being inhaled into the lungs.

The patient is also hooked up to an intravenous needle. An intravenous, or IV, infusion is often used with patients who are to undergo surgery. An IV is a clear plastic bag filled with glucose (a fluid nutrient-replenisher), to which a thin plastic tube is attached. This tube is joined to a needle and inserted into a vein, usually in the hand or inner elbow of the patient. While on an IV the patient is generally not allowed to eat but can receive a number of medications through the IV without any additional injections.

Before the surgery is to begin, the patient is given a drug to induce drowsiness (often through the IV tube) and is then transported to the operating room. As is the case in all surgical procedures, everything and everyone in this room conforms to the highest standard of cleanliness. Doctors and nurses scrub, or wash, and wear masks, gowns, and gloves to prevent the spreading of germs and infection that can prove so dangerous to a surgery patient. Once in the operating room, the anesthesiologist administers the anesthesia, which renders the patient unconscious during surgery. The anesthesiologist also keeps a close watch on the patient's breathing and heart function throughout the operation.

During transplant surgery, a heart-lung machine is used to pump blood throughout the recipient's body until the new heart can take over.

At about the same time the surgeons are making their first incision, the heart that has been donated arrives in the operating room in a plastic cooler. It has probably been transported in this cooler, sometimes over great distances, preserved by a device that pumps cool plasma (the clear, watery fluid that is the liquid part of blood) through the donated organ's blood vessels during the long trip and ensuing wait.

The surgeon begins the operation by making an incision, the two edges of which are held apart by curved instruments called protractors. To help control bleeding and ensure better visibility during the difficult task of reattaching an organ, a small suction tube is used to pull out blood. Electrocautery, a tiny burst of electrical current that seals off the bleeding vessel, is also employed. The patient's body is cooled down to approximately 77 degrees in order to reduce the body tissues' need for oxygen.

The surgeon then begins the procedure of removing the diseased organ. In heart transplant surgery this involves cutting through the ribs and keeping them apart with a device specially built to spread them. The lungs, which

Once the old heart is cut away and lifted out, surgeons at New York's Columbia Presbyterian Medical Center put a donated heart in place in the recipient's chest cavity.

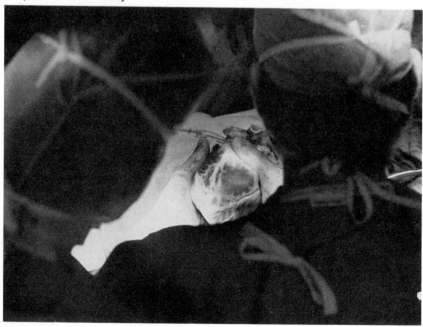

partially cover the heart, are pushed aside to make the heart more visible. The heart is then disconnected from its blood supply. The surgeon will sever the connecting blood vessels—which will be reattached to the new heart—and connect them to a heart-lung machine that will oxygenate and circulate the blood through the body until the new heart is in place. The surgeons cut the majority of the heart out, leaving in place the upper part of the upper two chambers, including the vena cava and pulmonary vein. Then the new heart is ready to be put in.

Putting in the new heart is both delicate and very difficult work. The new organ is sutured in, and each blood vessel must be painstakingly reattached so that blood circulation will be resumed and the organ will function properly. In order to make these connections perfectly, some surgeons use a magnifying glass, or even a microscope. Often, a magnifying device similar to goggles can be worn by the surgeon to ensure maximum visibility. Once the surgeon sews the heart in, he or she begins to warm both the heart and the recipient. The surgeon then shocks and stimulates the heart with drugs to start it beating again.

The patient is removed from the heart-lung machine to see if the new organ will work on its own. Once the blood is circulating freely through the new organ, the surgeon must secure the ribs together

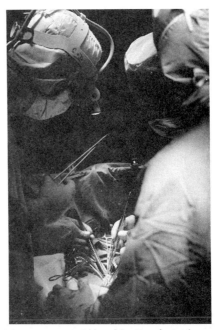

Surgeons at Columbia Presbyterian Medical Center use headgear that enables them to see and reattach microscopic blood vessels, thus ensuring proper blood flow through the new organ.

with metal clamps and close the incisions, both inside and out of the body. (Stitches inside the body will dissolve; those holding the outer layers of skin together will be removed at a later date.)

The patient is transferred to an intensive care unit where his or her condition is monitored for any signs of infection or rejection. Immediately after surgery, the patient will begin taking immunosuppressant drugs in order to reduce the chance of rejection. Although these drugs can prevent rejection

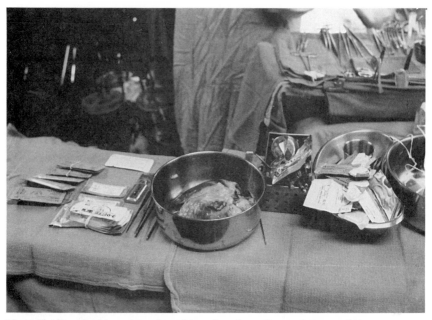

The old, diseased heart is placed in a bowl on the periphery of the operating area. In some cases, the heart is so damaged that the patient would have died within hours if a donated organ had not been found.

from taking place, they also leave the patient open to infection, which can prove fatal. In order to avoid this, the patient is placed in a private room, and all visitors are carefully screened and required to don protective clothing before entering. Once the immunosuppressant drugs are decreased in dosage, the rules are relaxed.

Patients who undergo organ-transplant surgery recuperate gradually and must remain on these immunosuppressant drugs for the rest of their life. If all goes well, they can return home just a few weeks after surgery. Many return to their jobs as well. Naturally, the complications are many, the adjustments often difficult, the failures terribly bitter; but as Donald DiMaggio, two-year survivor of heart-transplant surgery, recently said, it is often worth the risks. "Go for it," said DiMaggio. "I went for it—and I'm still here."

· · · · · · · · · · · · · ·

CHAPTER 5

A PATIENT'S POINT OF VIEW

A young dialysis patient

Organ-transplant surgery dramatically improves the health, quality of life, and life expectancy of many people whose organs have failed. But having this surgery and recovering from it is not easy. Patients who choose to undergo organ-transplant surgery confront a wide range of problems and face enormous changes and challenges in all areas of their life.

By the time transplant candidates receive a new kidney, for example, they have often been ill for years. They may be drained of physical and emotional energy. Many chronically ill patients have also become very dependent on parents or others for their most basic needs. Many patients may also be daunted by the challenges posed by organ transplantation. But because of the possible benefits they may gain from it they resolve to undergo organ-transplant surgery.

They must often wait—for months or even years—until a compatible organ is available. This period of seemingly endless waiting is often very tense, and precedes the stress and worry of facing the actual operation. The patient may find him- or herself worrying about surviving the operation, about the treatments he or she will have to undergo, about the discomfort and pain that may accompany and follow the operation, and about whether or not the transplant will be successful.

To further complicate matters, the medication many transplant patients receive after surgery, such as steroids and pain-killing drugs, may cause hallucinations, agitation, and other frightening emotional and mental disturbances. In some cases, patients may become so disoriented immediately after transplant surgery that antipsychotic medication must be prescribed for them.

Once these obstacles have been met, the patient's own high expectations may themselves cause severe emotional difficulties. People who are to receive kidney transplants, for example, often fantasize about how much better their life will be after the surgery and are bitterly disappointed when the new organ does not solve all of their medical problems. They may become very depressed when life with the transplanted organ does not match up with their idea of what it would be like.

If the transplanted organ comes from someone who has died— a cadaver donor—the person who receives it may also feel guilty that this person had to lose their life in order that the patient might gain life. If the wait for a suitable organ is prolonged, the patient may secretly wish for someone to die so that an organ will become available. While this wish is certainly an understandable one, the patient is likely to feel ashamed and guilty about it, even though there is no objective reason for doing so. And if the transplanted organ is rejected, the patient may feel even more guilty—for not being able to make it work, or for "wasting" the organ—and in addition may feel very angry at having gone through the whole transplant ordeal without being better off as a result of it.

All of these things are common experiences for organ-transplant patients, and may cause them to become depressed. They may be so upset that they become unable to sleep, eat, or enjoy any activities. Medical professionals recognize that the emotions of transplant patients are often in a constant upheaval and that it is normal for them to have feelings of fear, sadness, worry, concern, and even anger.

In light of this, many medical professionals offer their patients counseling, support, and the opportunity to express fears and worries. But when these measures are not enough, psychiatric treatment may be needed in order to help transplant patients understand and deal with their feelings. Sometimes, psychiatric drugs may be prescribed to help these patients recover from their emotional distress and begin feeling better. And some patients need counseling for emotional distress even after they leave the hospital.

Once transplant patients do return home, they may be confronted by long-term problems and adjustments that could cause them further psychological troubles. We have already mentioned

Chaplain Randy Roberts counsels the family of a transplant patient at Loma Linda University Medical Center in Loma Linda, California.

Heart-transplant recipient Jim Hayes (right) exercises his new heart. Transplant patients must have a positive mental outlook and be prepared to make the transition from disabling illness to a healthy, active life.

the potential side effects of steroids, drugs that are taken in conjunction with cyclosporine. These can result in marked changes in the patient's appearance; for example, the patient's face may become round, with fattened cheeks, and excess growth of facial and body hair is often noted. These sorts of alterations are especially upsetting to young people, many of whom are insecure about their appearance to begin with.

Steroids may also cause a brittleness and fragility of the bones that restricts physical activities; in addition steroids can cause feelings of depression, with symptoms ranging from mild unhappiness to severe emotional misery and suicidal thoughts.

Beyond the difficulties posed by the surgery and medication, post-transplant patients face the challenge of returning to as normal a life as possible. Adult transplant recipients must, for instance, balance the benefits of returning to work, if they are able to do so, against the likelihood that they will lose government health-care benefits should they begin earning much money on their own. Students face the curiosity, and sometimes the insensitivity, of classmates.

In addition, young people must meet the usual challenges of growing up and establishing their independence. For young transplant recipients this is made especially difficult by the fact that they have grown accustomed to being dependent on others, and that their parents are likely to be even more protective than most parents.

In short, all post-transplant patients must somehow make the change, as much as is possible, from "sick person" to "well person." And they must do this while continuing to face physical problems and knowing that, no matter how much time passes, their new organ may still be rejected.

A CASE HISTORY

What is it really like to face the challenges of organ transplant surgery? And why would anyone want to undergo organ transplantation at all, if it is so difficult?

Karen Feeley knows the answers to those questions. Karen is a pretty, petite young woman in her mid-twenties, with blond hair, bright eyes, and an enthusiastic smile. She recently began working at a new job as an accountant for a large business. Karen likes clothes and music, and on weekends enjoys going out with her friends. In fact, Karen is much like many other young adults, except that on June 1, 1987, she underwent kidney-transplant surgery for the second time.

Three months after the surgery, Karen sat at the kitchen table in her Waterbury, Connecticut home and answered questions about her experiences before, during, and after receiving her new kidney.

How did you come to need a kidney transplant?

"This all started about three-and-a-half years ago. I have lupus erythematosus [an inflammatory disease that damages body tissues], a disease which can cause kidney damage. So I knew I might get kidney failure, but I didn't know it had happened until my doctor called and asked me to come in for an appointment— and to bring my mother along. I knew then something was wrong. As it turned out, blood tests had shown my kidneys weren't working."

Did you start on kidney dialysis right away?

"Yes. First they put me in the hospital, and I had surgery on my arm to strengthen the blood vessels in it. Each time you have dialysis, they have to put two needles in your arm. Having that done several times a week, every week, would ruin the vessels unless they did surgery to strengthen them in advance. Here, feel my wrist."

On Karen's wrist, where the bump-bump-bump of the pulse is usually felt, there is instead a humming, buzzing feeling. To get blood out of the body, through the dialysis machine, and back into the body, it is necessary to put a needle into a blood vessel in the wrist. But puncturing the vessel several times a week for dialysis would destroy it, unless it were artificially strengthened. To strengthen the vessel, surgeons create a *subcutaneous* (under the skin) *arteriovenous* (artery to vein) *shunt*—that is, they connect a large artery to a large vein in the wrist. (An artery is a blood vessel that carries blood at high pressure from the heart

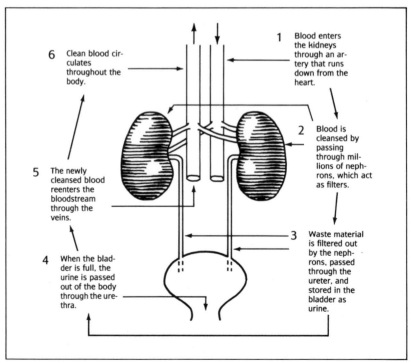

6 Clean blood circulates throughout the body.

1 Blood enters the kidneys through an artery that runs down from the heart.

2 Blood is cleansed by passing through millions of nephrons, which act as filters.

5 The newly cleansed blood reenters the bloodstream through the veins.

3 Waste material is filtered out by the nephrons, passed through the ureter, and stored in the bladder as urine.

4 When the bladder is full, the urine is passed out of the body through the urethra.

Figure 2: How The Kidneys Function. *Although most humans are born with two kidneys, only one is needed to remove waste from the body.*

out to the body. A vein is a vessel that carries blood at lower pressure from the body back to the heart.) Once this has been done, high-pressure arterial blood can enter the vein; the higher pressure causes the vein to enlarge and develop a thicker, stronger wall that will not be destroyed by repeated puncture. Sometimes surgeons connect the vein and artery directly; sometimes they use a connecting tube made of Gore-tex, Teflon, or Dacron. These materials are used because they are smooth; thus few blood cells snag on the inside of tubes made from them (snags would cause blood clots and block off the shunt). After the shunt has been made, the artery's blood no longer flows directly into the hand; instead, some flows across the shunt into the vein. This causes the normal bump-bump of the artery's pulse to smooth out into a steadier buzzing feeling.

"That's from the blood-vessel surgery," Karen explained. "After it was done, I had dialysis three times a week. When I first started, I went during the day; later, when I was working again, I went

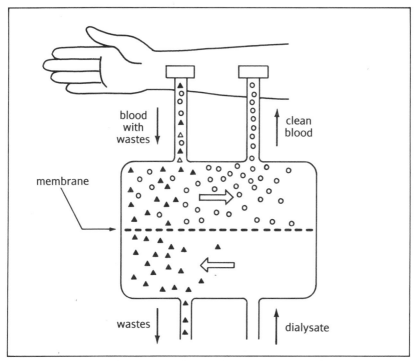

Figure 3: Hemodialysis. *Many kidney-failure patients, like Karen Feeley, must undergo some type of dialysis several times a week.*

after work, Monday, Wednesday, and Friday evenings, four hours each time."

How did you feel the first time you went for dialysis?

"Petrified. Like a scared little kid. I didn't know anything about it at all. But it was not as frightening as I thought it would be. There was a guy my age there, and he came up to me and talked about it. That helped me through it.

"One of the worst things was that the other people there were much older than I was. They looked frail, really sick, and it scared me—I wondered if I would get to be like that. Later I found out many of them had other, worse illnesses than I did— other things wrong, besides their kidneys. But when I started having dialysis in the evenings, there were more people my age there—a livelier crowd. That was better."

Exactly how does a person get connected to a dialysis machine?

"First they give you two shots of Novocain [a painkilling drug] in your arm. Then they put in two needles, each attached to a tube. Your blood comes out one needle, goes through the tube into the machine, gets cleaned in there, and comes out the other tubing, back into you."

Were there any physical side effects from being on dialysis?

"For me, not too many. Sometimes I felt sick when I was coming off it, but during it, I usually slept. Some other people felt quite ill from dialysis sometimes, though."

How long was it before the idea of a kidney transplant was first suggested and what did you think of the idea?

"Transplant was suggested almost immediately. And I felt I really didn't have a choice—or, rather, I had a choice, but it wasn't a good one. I just thought, do I want to get hooked up to a dialysis machine every other night, or do I want to be able to do all the things I want to do instead?

"You see, the worst thing about dialysis isn't the needles or anything like that, the way you might think. The worst thing is, if you work or go to school, dialysis takes up all the rest of your time. I was always telling my friends I couldn't do things with them because I had to have dialysis. I didn't go on vacation for the same reason. I crammed all the things I wanted to do into Tuesday and Thursday nights, and I slept the weekends away just because I was so exhausted.

"So I signed up for the transplant program, and just a few months later they called me."

When they called and said, "We've got a kidney for you," were you ready? Did you already have your bags all packed, waiting for the call?

"Oh, no. They had said I might wait two weeks for a kidney, or I might wait two years. It could be any time. When they did call, it was midnight on a Saturday night, and my dad thought at first it was a crank call, someone playing a joke. But at seven o'clock the next morning, there I was at the hospital.

"And of course I was nervous, but not too nervous. I remember lying on a stretcher outside the operating room, waiting to be taken in, and a man went by carrying a cooler, the kind they use to transport organs. I called out, 'Hey, is that my kidney?' And it could have been. Really, I just wanted to get it over with, see if it would work."

But the first one didn't work, did it?

"At first it did. They called me 'Wonder Girl,' because it worked so well. But then after about twenty days, my body rejected it, and it had to be removed. And I had other complications too. A

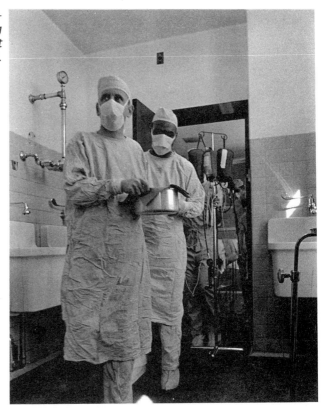

A donor kidney is transported to the operating room where a recipient awaits a transplant.

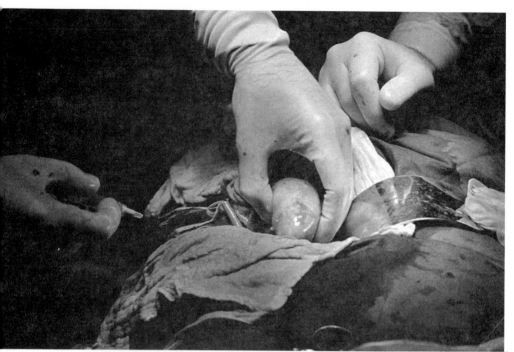

A donated kidney is placed into the recipient by the transplant surgeon. After placement, the kidney's blood vessels are attached to those in the recipient's body, to ensure proper blood flow through the organ.

lot of things went wrong, and when it was all over I went back on dialysis again. I stayed on dialysis for more than a year."

Were you discouraged?

"Very. I said I would never go through it again, I wouldn't try another transplant. But later I changed my mind."

While all this was going on—having to be on dialysis, and then having your transplant—did you feel that people treated you differently?

"Definitely. Yes. It was as if they were scared of me. My coworkers, some of my friends—it was as if they thought they might catch something from me. When I was on dialysis, my arm was much bumpier than it is now. The veins were lumpy from having the needles in them. It made me look different. And people seemed afraid to touch me—that buzzing feeling in my wrist, for example. They'd be curious so I'd say, 'Go ahead and touch it.' But they'd jump when they did. I handled that by making a joke of it; I'd say, 'It's because I'm bionic.'

"Also, it seemed some people were watching for something bad to happen. They'd say, 'How are you?' I'd say, 'Fine.' And they'd answer, 'No, *really*, how are you?' I knew it was because they cared, but—anyway, a lot of people did treat me differently, still do, and it's sometimes hard to handle. But I've adjusted; you just learn how to handle these things after a while."

How did you decide to try having a transplant a second time?

"I had another friend on dialysis, who persuaded me to sign up again. Actually, he told me. He said, 'You're signing up.' He took me to the hospital to get on the waiting list for a new kidney, and really urged me. And again, it didn't take long before the hospital called me."

How long were you in the hospital after you had the second transplant?

"Seven and a half weeks. That was hard. The first month I kept my spirits up, but after that I sometimes got depressed about having to be there. I felt good, but I couldn't leave because I kept getting infections, or something would happen that had to be treated there.

"So I got dressed every day in regular clothes, not a hospital gown or nightgown. If I didn't get dressed, that meant I felt really low.

"I'd go outside, walk around, go to the gift shop. I was there so long I started answering the phones at the nursing desk! But it was always on my mind—worrying that the transplant wasn't going to work; wondering why I kept getting infections—that was scary."

So now you've been home about a month, and you are still under your doctor's care, and you take antirejection medication, right?

"Right. I go in to have my blood samples taken three times a week. And I take prednisone and cyclosporine. Ten prednisone pills in the morning, four in the afternoon, plus the cyclosporine twice a day. You take cyclosporine by mixing it in warm fruit juice and drinking it."

What side effects are there from these drugs?

"The side effects are the most difficult part of this. The prednisone makes my face fat, I just hate that, and it makes my stomach stick out. And it makes me want to eat when I'm not really hungry. I've started learning to look at a piece of food and say, 'No, I don't want that.' But it's hard, especially having the fat face.

"You see, my face never looked like this before. It really has gotten fat because of the medication. People who knew me before don't even recognize me, and some of them say things. Last week I ran into a guy I'd known before, and he must have said five times, 'I didn't know it was you—you got so fat.' That night I came home practically in tears.

"On the other hand, some people say I look good, and many people who didn't know me before don't even notice. One guy I worked with was very natural about it. Just came up to me, asked me how I was doing. Later he told me he was amazed at the change in my appearance, but he was so good about the way he approached me.

"Sometimes also my hands shake, and my muscle tone is flabbier. I should start exercising. The cyclosporine sometimes makes my bones ache. And I have a lot more hair—on my body, and also on my face. I bleach the hair on my face, so it's not noticeable. Those are all effects of the drugs."

What about good things that have come from the surgery? What do you get that compensates for the drugs' side effects?

"I have so much energy I don't know what to do! I have tons of energy. I'm always going out, making plans. Maybe I'll slow down when the newness wears off, but now I'm just so excited to be able to do things, so glad just to feel good."

If a person, especially a young person who was trying to decide whether to have a transplant, asked you for your advice, what would you say?

"I'd say do it. You really have no choice, if you want a normal life. People sometimes tell me I'm so brave, and I say, 'You'd do it too, if you were in this predicament.' It's not bravery, it's just, do you want to spend half your life hooked up to a dialysis machine? I'd say do it, you should definitely have the transplant."

You really seem to have a good handle on the whole situation. You even make it sound easy, but I'm sure it hasn't all been easy.

"No. It isn't all easy. I mean, sometimes I sit at this kitchen table and cry, but no one sees it. I think, 'Why did this all have to happen to me? Other people don't have things like this happen.' I even think—and I don't like to admit this—'why couldn't it have happened to someone else instead?' But then I think, 'Stop feeling sorry for yourself. There are a lot of worse things.' I mean, I could have had to have a heart transplant. I got one of the easier ones."

What's your advice on how to behave toward someone who's had a transplant?

"Just act the same way you've always acted toward them. If you want to ask them questions, ask—people who've had transplants aren't scared to answer. I'll talk about it to anyone who asks— I'm glad if someone wants to know."

Have you learned things from having a kidney transplant that you would not have learned otherwise?

"In addition to the physical benefits I have from the new kidney, I also think the experience has made me much more mature. I've grown up a lot through it. Before surgery, I might have made fun of someone who had a fat face like I have now—just thoughtlessly. I was more likely to judge a book by its cover, you know?

"But not any more. Now I think, 'Give the person a chance.' The person might have a good reason for the way they look or for whatever is different about them—medical problems or personal problems. I understand a little better now. You see things differently when you have some of these problems yourself. I see things differently because of what has happened to me."

Sandimmune, or cyclosporine, is mixed with fruit juice and taken orally to combat organ-transplant rejection.

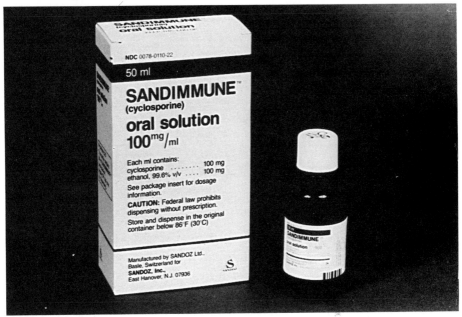

In Karen's kitchen, the telephone rings; she answers. It is one of her co-workers at her new job, wanting to know how her doctor's appointment went today, and if she will be at work tomorrow.

Karen tells the caller that the appointment went fine, and yes, she'll be at work tomorrow. Later, she tells her co-worker that she wants to go shopping, and that this coming weekend she will be going to the Eastern States Exposition—a big state fair.

Hanging up the telephone, Karen smiles: a big, enthusiastic smile. Happy and full of energy and plans for the future, Karen Feeley knows better than most people that organ transplantation has its down side. But since her kidney transplant, Karen is able to do the things she plans—which is why she refuses to let the down side keep her down for very long.

•   •   •   •

CHAPTER 6

· · · · · · · · · · · · · · · ·

ETHICAL ISSUES

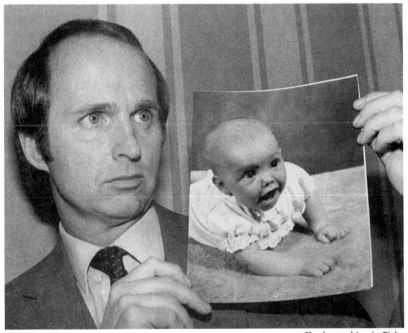

Charles and Jamie Fiske

The success of organ transplants has raised issues that have never had to be faced before. A case in point is that of an 11-month-old Bridgewater, Massachusetts, girl named Jamie Fiske. In 1982, Jamie received the liver of a 10-month-old Utah boy who had been killed only hours earlier in a car accident. The surgery went well. It looked as if Jamie, who would have soon died without a new liver, now had an excellent chance to live.

The news of Jamie's good fortune was reported on radio and television and in newspapers all over the country. But along with good wishes from many people who had been following the story of Jamie's wait for a liver transplant, the news also brought criticism and questions.

Why, people asked, did Jamie Fiske get the liver? After all, while Jamie was very sick, many other children in the country needed a new liver, too. People wanted to know—why Jamie Fiske?

Part of the reason lay in the publicity that had surrounded Jamie's desperate need for the transplant; publicity that Jamie Fiske's father had deliberately provoked. A hospital administrator, Charles Fiske had telephoned hundreds of doctors around the country, alerting them to his child's need for a new liver. He wrote to Senator Edward Kennedy and Speaker of the House of Representatives Thomas O'Neill. In New York, Fiske addressed the annual convention of the American Academy of Pediatrics, one of the few nonphysicians ever to be granted that privilege.

News of all his activity soon began appearing in the media, just as Fiske intended; the more people who knew about Jamie's plight, he realized, the sooner a liver might be found for her. "I ask you to keep your eyes and ears open for a donor," he begged in *Time* magazine. "Jamie wants to live." Soon CBS newsman Dan Rather picked up the story and told of Jamie's plight on nationwide television.

As a result of all this, the parents of the 10-month-old baby in Utah remembered Jamie when they lost their own child, and decided they wanted to donate his liver to her. In this way, they felt, their child's tragic death might have some meaning. The two children's tissues matched, and little Jamie received the organ.

After the transplant, however, many people questioned the means by which Jamie had received her new liver. Everyone understood that Jamie's father was only doing his best for his child, but they also knew that he had used resources to which most people do not have access. Some parents of other children who needed transplants were bitter. Perhaps, they said, if they were hospital administrators who knew their way around the medical bureaucracy and the news media and could influence it as Charles Fiske had, their own children would not still be waiting for organs.

The controversy that surrounded the case brought to light one of the most critical social problems created by medicine's ability to transplant human organs: There are simply not enough donated organs for all the people who need them.

According to the Task Force on Transplantation created by the U.S. Congress, more than 20,000 people in the United States could be organ donors each year. (These are people who die from causes that do not damage their organs, such as head injuries.) Yet of these 20,000, only about 3,000 are organ donors.

Knowing that there is a serious organ shortage and that there are guidelines to determine who receives each available organ, is it ethically right to advertise for an organ, as Charles Fiske did? Is it right for relatives of donors to say who gets the donor's organs when they die, as the Utah boy's parents did? When a suitable organ becomes available, but two or more patients need it, should it go to a poor mother of three who is living on welfare,

A poster distributed by the American Liver Foundation of Wisconsin is just one example of the many efforts that are being made to increase organ donation.

or to a wealthy businessman? To the one who has received a lot of publicity, or to one who waits in silence?

In 1987, the U.S. government passed a law designed to make sure these kinds of decisions are made fairly. It requires the nation's approximately 200 transplant centers (medical centers where transplant operations are performed) to disregard patients' publicity campaigns, the wishes of donors, and other factors such as a patient's ability to pay for a transplant. Instead, the centers were told to choose organ recipients via the computerized, nationwide system described earlier. This system, run through UNOS, was developed by transplant pioneer Dr. Thomas Starzl.

But even with these new requirements, the issue has not really been decided. Although some transplant centers agree with the idea of a computerized system for matching organs and recipients, others feel that families do have a right to campaign for their members, and that this aggressiveness should be allowed. These same transplant centers also feel that the wishes of the family of a deceased person should be honored, even if they include donating an organ to a specific recipient. Moreover, the new law requiring computerized donor/recipient matching clashes with some state laws that require organs donated within a certain state to go only to residents of that state. It would appear that medical progress in organ transplantation has moved faster than law and social policy.

Procuring More Organs

The problem of deciding who gets which organ would not be so severe if more organs were available for transplantation. Although some people believe that organ donation should be mandatory, most of society holds that people have the right to decide what is done with their body, even after death. Organ donation, most people believe, must remain voluntary.

An attempt to voluntarily enlarge the supply of organs for transplantation was begun in 1967, when the federal government enacted the Uniform Anatomical Gift Act. This law allows individuals to donate organs in advance of their death by signing a Uniform Donor Card. Many states now also ask driver's license applicants to indicate on their license whether or not they wish to be a donor.

Unfortunately, the Uniform Anatomical Gift Act did not solve the organ-shortage problem, for even now that it is fairly easy to become an organ donor, many people do not. Some people are put off by the idea that parts of their body will be removed, even if it is after death. Indeed, one of the main reasons for the shortage of organ donors is simply that many healthy people find it difficult to think about death at all. They may prefer to pretend to themselves that they will never die, or they may mean to donate their organs but "never quite get around to it."

Others really would like to donate their organs but do not know how.

Approaching the Family

When people who have not donated their organs in advance die suddenly, a difficult situation often arises. The federal government requires that hospitals receiving federal funds ask patients or their family about organ donation whenever organs are, or are about to become, available. But asking families to donate the organs of their dying loved ones is hard for hospital professionals, because it increases the distress of people who are already very upset.

Typically, the family arrives at the hospital to find their critically injured loved one being supported by a respirator—a machine that maintains the breathing of a seriously injured person. The doctors may say that the injured person is brain dead—which means that there is no hope at all for recovery of any kind. Still, the person's organs may give someone else a chance to live.

Naturally, when a person's heart still beats and a machine supplies oxygen to that person's lungs, his or her loved ones do not want to accept the idea that for all intents and purposes, death has occurred. Yet once the brain has died, the person has died too, even though that person's other organs may continue, with artificial help, to work for a long enough period to allow them to be transplanted.

It is in this setting that hospital personnel must ask families to donate their loved ones' organs. To wait until the injured person's heart finally stops beating on its own would mean not only prolonging the family's anguish, but risking crucial damage to the transplantable organs of someone whose death is certain to occur in any case.

Therefore, grieving families are forced to choose: Should they let artificial life-support systems such as respirators be turned off in order to allow organs to be removed from a loved one who has suffered brain death? Can they feel sure that doctors have done everything possible for the dying patient before removing his or her organs so that they can be given to help someone else to live? People who are not in such difficult circumstances also wonder about donating organs. Can they feel safe in directing that their own organs be transplanted, if such a fate should ever come to them?

The answer to all of these questions is yes: Physicians always do everything possible to save a life before removing organs for transplantation. Most states have enacted laws stating that brain death shall be declared and organs removed for transplantation only when all functions of the brain have irreversibly stopped. Furthermore, the physicians taking care of a patient who has suffered brain death are not the same ones caring for the patient who needs a transplant. They make the diagnosis of brain death on the basis of medical fact, not in the light of someone else's need for a transplanted organ.

Families who have faced the tragic situation of having to decide whether or not to donate a relative's organs, and who have done so, often derive comfort later from the knowledge that their loved one has helped others. Said one such family, "Our miracle didn't happen. Our son died. Days later, we realized that miracles were happening for other people. [Our son's] life had a purpose. He left a wonderful legacy. He was able to give life to others."

Other families, however, hesitate to donate their loved ones' organs on religious grounds. All major religions, however, condone organ transplantation. Some families are concerned that the removal of bones, skin, or organs will prevent them from holding an open-casket wake for the deceased. This also is untrue; bones can be replaced by artificial bones, and neither organs nor skin grafts that have been removed from the body of a deceased person are noticeable to the eye. But even when all of these questions have been resolved, the sad fact is that many physicians and other health-care personnel simply do not ask the family of a fatally ill or brain dead person whether they have considered

After being unemployed for more than 3 months, in 1975 Aaron Rowe, 39, made a controversial offer to sell a kidney or an eye for $10,000. The issue of buying and selling organs raises a number of ethical questions that have yet to be addressed.

organ donation. Put off by the emotional undercurrents, or overwhelmed by other responsibilities, these professionals allow many potential organs for donation to go unused.

Selling Spare Parts

Because of the constant shortage of organs for transplantation, people sometimes try to profit by selling their organs, much as some people donate blood to get money. Needless to say, regardless of whether or not someone allowed this, it would not be possible for any of that person's vital organs to be removed without resulting in his or her death, and possible murder charges against the surgeon who removed the organs. In the case of organs that can be removed without harming the donor, however, the question of whether or not it is legal and ethical to sell these organs does come into play.

Kidneys, corneas, bones, and bone marrow are some of the organs that can be removed, without immediate harm, from a living donor; these body parts are in great demand by persons anxiously awaiting transplants. Some patients waiting for kidneys or other organs are desperate enough to pay almost any price for them. The legal questions raised by the possibility of such sales, however, are staggering. For example, what if the organ does not work? Does the recipient get a refund? If the donor were to change his mind, could he sue to get the organ back?

In addition to the problems raised by the shortage of organs for transplantation, the problem of who is obligated to pay for transplants is a serious one. In 1987, the average cost of a kidney transplant was more than $30,000. Costs for more complicated transplants, and for drugs necessary for the treatment of persons who have received transplants, were even higher; a heart transplant may cost more than $200,000 and a liver transplant even more.

Not many people can afford to pay so much money by themselves, and because in our society medical care is believed to be a right, not a privilege, a percentage of the cost is usually borne by insurance companies and, to an increasing degree, by the government. In the meantime, the cost of organ transplantation is increasing steadily. In 1975, for example, the Federal Health

In 1984 Dr. Leonard L. Bailey, heart-transplant surgeon at Loma Linda University Medical Center in Loma Linda, California, transplanted the heart of a baboon into an infant, Baby Fae. The infant lived for 20 days after the surgery.

Care Finance Administration put the cost of nationwide health care at $132.7 billion, or about $590 for each person. Ten years later, in 1985, the cost of health care had risen $425 billion, or $1,721 per person. While not all of the increase was due to organ transplants, growing numbers of these very expensive procedures certainly contribute to escalating health-care costs.

A related problem of special importance to organ-transplant recipients is the cost of their care after transplant surgery. As we have already seen, treatment with the anti-rejection medication cyclosporine can cost more than $12,000 per year. At the same time, however, many organ recipients cannot get jobs because their history of illness disqualifies them from being included in business-sponsored health-insurance plans.

Thus, many organ recipients not only become unable to pay their medical bills, but must exhaust their savings and eventually turn to welfare simply to get by. Not all organ recipients have such problems, but according to one patient who wants to work but cannot get hired for this reason, having had an organ transplant is "like having the plague."

Animal-to-Human Transplants

In 1984, Dr. Leonard L. Bailey transplanted the heart of a baboon into an infant girl, who was given the pseudonym Baby Fae, at the Loma Linda University Medical Center in Loma Linda, California. Baby Fae lived for 20 days after the surgery before succumbing to the rejection process. The revolutionary surgery touched off a furor of debate, as scientists and surgeons around the world questioned Dr. Bailey's use of animal organs for transplantation to a human being.

Although no such transplants have taken place since that time, many organ-transplant surgeons, including Dr. Bailey himself, believe that animal-to-human transplants can serve as a bridge for an organ recipient until a suitable human organ can be found.

Furthermore, according to a December 15, 1987, article in the *New York Times*, Dr. Bailey felt that "Baby Fae started a new era in heart transplantation" because during the operation he was able to utilize on an infant the transplant skills he had developed working on adults. Such an operation requires great precision because of the small size and weight of the infant heart. Since that landmark operation, Dr. Bailey has been able to successfully

Doctors Elmar P. Sakala (left) and Joyce Peabody announce in 1987 that an anencephalic baby, who was to be the first anencephalic infant carried to term for the purpose of organ donation, was stillborn.

perform heart-transplant operations on a number of infants, using hearts from infants who have died from other causes.

The Debate Over Anencephalic Babies

Anencephalic babies are babies born with most of their brain missing as a result of failure to develop normally in the womb. Unless they are hooked to a respirator, these infants usually die within hours of birth. According to a December 7, 1987, article in the *New York Times*, nearly 3,500 anencephalic infants are born in the United States each year; with the exception of the brain, all of their organs are intact and can give life to 4 or 5 infants awaiting transplant.

In 1987, Brenda and Michael Winner were expecting their first child. Shortly into the pregnancy, however, it was discovered through prenatal testing that the child would be born anencephalic. Devastated by this tragedy, the Winners nonetheless decided to carry the child to full term and, upon its birth, to donate its organs. This decision proved to be a difficult one because no hospital was willing to accept the child for transplantation of its organs.

Finally, after waging a national battle to have their child's organs donated, the Winners were able to persuade Loma Linda University Medical Center to accept the child. This decision, which led to the creation of a special ward for anencephalic infants who were to be kept alive until their organs were transplanted, opened up new options to the parents of such infants, and will enable many more infant-organ transplants to take place.

Unfortunately, the Winner's daughter was stillborn, and her organs could not be donated.

In February of 1988, however, the first anencephalic organ donor to be admitted to the special ward at Loma Linda University Medical Center was born and was put on life-support systems to await the transplantation of his organs.

Baby Jesse is held by his grandfather at a party celebrating his first anniversary with his new heart. In a controversial decision, Jesse was first denied the operation because his parents were not married.

The use of anencephalic infants for organ donations has touched off a debate within the medical community. Although some people feel that putting these infants on respirators makes it more difficult to determine the exact moment at which they become brain dead, others feel that letting them die naturally wastes a large number of organs that are desperately needed by the many infants awaiting transplants. Refusing to accept the donation of the organs of anencephalic infants also denies the parents of such infants the opportunity to donate their child's organs and in some way compensate for their tragedy.

At this time, with several transplant operations already performed using the organs of anencephalic infants, it would appear that the parents of such infants will continue to have the right to donate their child's organs, and that surgeons who specialize in infant transplants will have a new and larger donor group from which to take organs for infants who need them.

Like many of the issues now being considered about organ transplants, this too may change. The important point is that as technology becomes more sophisticated and enables us to expand and perfect both our system of organ donation and our surgical techniques for transplanting organs, so must our laws and ethical codes grow to meet the demands of these advances. When there is a balance between ethics and technology, all of us may be confident that should we someday require an organ transplant, we will receive both the medical care and the support that we need.

•　　　•　　　•　　　•

CHAPTER 7

. . . .

THE FUTURE OF ORGAN TRANS-PLANTATION

Cesar Milstein

Some day, continuing research and efforts in the area of disease prevention may make many organ transplants unnecessary. For although some organ failures are unavoidable, many are not. Cigarette smoking may cause lung failure, for example, and alcohol and drug abuse can destroy the liver. Many preventable factors, among them fatty diet, obesity, and lack of exercise, can contribute to or even cause heart failure.

In the event that organs do fail, medicine and science have come a long way in the search for safe, effective ways to replace those organs. Today, thousands of transplants are performed each year, giving a new lease on life and its pleasures to many organ recipients. At the same time, research continues to seek even better methods to help people who need transplants, including antirejection drugs that are more effective and cause fewer unwanted side effects; better surgical techniques; and even artificial organs or spare parts that can improve the quality of life for those who receive them.

Recent Transplant and Implant Advances

One recent advance in the area of antirejection drugs is the development of Orthoclone OKT3. Produced by the Ortho Pharmaceutical Corporation, Orthoclone OKT3 consists of *monoclonal antibodies*. Monoclonal antibodies were first produced through a technique perfected at Cambridge University by Cesar Milstein and Georges J. F. Kohler, who in 1984 shared the Nobel Prize in medicine for their work.

These laboratory-made antibodies combat the body's own antitransplant reaction, leaving the rest of the immune system intact. Although the way in which they do this is still not completely

In March of 1987, in the first brain-graft surgery performed in the United States, Dickeye Baggett (center) received an adrenal-gland-cell transplant to combat Parkinson's disease.

understood, it is believed that monoclonal antibodies find and deactivate a certain structure called a T-cell antigen receptor on the surface of the T-lymphocyte. Once this structure is deactivated, the T-cell lymphocyte no longer attacks the transplanted organ. In its first clinical use, Orthoclone OKT3 prevented rejection of kidney transplants in 94% of the people who were treated with this antibody drug, a significant improvement over earlier kinds of rejection treatment, which could stop rejection in only 75% of the people treated with them.

Monoclonal antibodies are currently made from animal tissue, which limits their usefulness to a period of only about 10 days. After that, the body begins to recognize these antibodies as invaders, and neutralizes them. In the future, scientists hope to make monoclonal antibodies from human-tissue sources, increasing their safety and effectiveness.

Intensive studies are also in progress to find better surgical techniques for organ transplantation. Pancreas transplants, for example, could help an estimated 5,000 people in the United States today, but the operation is performed infrequently because it is very difficult for surgeons to transplant the pancreas without damaging it.

Nerve transplants may also become possible in the future if methods of connecting severed nerves can be perfected. Doctors Louis de Medinacelli and W. J. Freed, at the National Institute of Mental Health in Bethesda, Maryland, have restored movement to the legs of animals whose nerves had been cut, and Dr. Albert Aguayo at McGill University in Montreal has succeeded in restoring sight to fish and amphibians whose optic nerves had been severed. According to Dr. Aguayo, this work is "pure experiment . . . far away from being directly relevant to [use in people]." But such experimentation may someday prove tremendously useful to people who suffer nerve injuries.

Another exciting possibility is that of cell transplantation. In the future, it may be necessary to transplant only a tiny bit of pancreas tissue, for example, rather than a whole organ, to restore the production of insulin and other functions performed by the pancreas, in patients who have diabetes and other diseases in which the pancreas does not work normally. The technique has shown some promise when used in diabetic patients. Cell transplantation is also being investigated as a way to cure diseases that do not cause the failure of entire organs.

The work of Dr. Ignacio Madroza, a neurosurgeon at the La Raza Medical Center in Mexico City, is a case in point. In 1986, he reported transplanting cells from the adrenal gland of a human patient into the same patient's brain, in an attempt to treat a crippling brain disorder called Parkinson's disease.

First described by British physician James Parkinson in 1817, Parkinson's disease causes severe trembling and stiffness in the limbs, and a rolling movement of the body. The disease occurs when cells in a part of the brain called the *substantia nigra* stop producing the chemical substance known as *dopamine*. (Dopamine is a neurotransmitter, or chemical messenger, that is needed for nerve cells to start and stop muscle movements.) A synthetic, dopaminelike chemical called L-dopa can be given to patients with Parkinson's disease, but does not always remain effective, and in some cases, its side effects can be worse than the effects of Parkinson's disease. The side effects include spasms, nausea, and severe mental disturbances.

Noting that dopamine is also produced by the adrenal gland (a small organ located above the kidney), Madroza theorized that if cells from this gland were moved to a patient's brain, the cells might react with other brain cells to produce dopamine in the brain. Experiments proved that this was true. By the end of 1987, close to 200 patients had undergone adrenal-to-brain grafts or were getting ready to have this surgery. While the long-term results of such surgery are still not certain, cell transplantation of this type, if it proves to be effective, would offer new hope to thousands crippled not only by Parkinson's disease, but also by other disorders such as epilepsy and Alzheimer's disease.

Thanks to research on the complex inner workings of cells, transplanting only part of a cell—such as its genes, rather than whole cells, tissues, or organs—may also prove to be of immense benefit to patients who have genetic (inherited) diseases.

Genes, made up of the substance known as *deoxyribonucleic acid* (DNA), are the instruction books of cells; they tell cells what to do and how to do it. When the DNA of a sperm or egg cell is damaged, the disease that this damage causes may be passed on to a person's children; this is why some diseases (such as sickle-cell anemia, cystic fibrosis, Tay-Sachs disease, and others) run in families.

Through research into *recombinant DNA* techniques, which involve the replacement or modification of part of the DNA molecule, ways of inserting new and healthy genes into cells may be developed, and genetic diseases may eventually be prevented or cured.

Artificial organs also continue to be developed and perfected. Electronic devices that stimulate the heartbeat or make it regular, or which stimulate the phrenic nerve (the nerve that makes us breathe), are already providing better health to some people. And pumps implanted in the body can perform the functions of some organs by dispensing needed substances such as insulin in persons with diabetes, for example, as well as painkilling medication in people who suffer from cancer or other diseases. Two of the newest synthetic body parts now being readied for general use are artificial skin for severely burned patients, and an artificial inner-ear device to help the deaf to hear.

Heart-transplant recipient Jason Lewis, 13, enjoys the freedom of an active, relatively normal life.

It is likely, however, that the need for real organs for transplantation will continue into the future. Thus, the scarcity of donated organs remains a serious problem. More would be available if organs from brain-dead or cadaver donors could be preserved longer. In this regard, a new preserving solution developed by University of Wisconsin scientists James Southard and Folkert O. Belzer promises to significantly increase the amount of time donated organs can be safely stored.

These are just a few of the areas in which the field of organ transplantation is moving forward daily. So much is being discovered and implemented, in fact, that by the time this book reaches its readers, more advances are sure to have been made.

As a result of these advances, today's teenagers have a better chance of surviving serious disease or injury—perhaps through a successful organ transplant—than at any other time in history. And a few years from now, when today's teenagers begin raising their own family, their children's prospects for life and health will be even more improved through one of modern medicine's newest and brightest miracles: organ transplantation.

•　　　•　　　•　　　•

APPENDIX 1: FOR MORE INFORMATION

The following is a list of national organizations that can provide additional information on transplantation or recommend other agencies that can be of further assistance.

American Council on
  Transplantation (ACT)
700 North Fairfax, Suite 505
Alexandria, VA 22314
(703) 836-4301
(800) ACT-GIVE

American Society for Artificial
  Internal Organs, Inc.
P.O. Box "C"
Boca Raton, FL 33429
(305) 391-8589

Children's Transplant Association
  (CTA)
P.O. Box 2106
Laurinburg, NC 28352
(919) 276-7171

The Living Bank (LB)
P.O. Box 6725
Houston, TX 77265
(800) 528-2971

Medic Alert Organ Donor Program
P.O. Box 1009
Tunock, CA 95381
(209) 668-3333
(800) ID ALERT

National Association of Patients on
  Hemodialysis and
  Transplantation, Inc.
150 Nassau Street
New York, NY 10038
(212) 619-2727

National Organ Transplant
  Education Foundation (NOTEF)
1275 K Street N.W.
Suite 900
Washington, D.C. 20005
(203) 371-0393

North American Transplant
  Coordinators Organization
  (NATCO)
5000 Van Nuys Boulevard
Suite 400
Sherman Oaks, CA 90405
(818) 995-7338

Organ Recovery (OR)
1909 East 101st Street
Cleveland, OH 44106
(216) 791-5433

Pittsburgh Transplant Foundation
5743 Center Avenue
Pittsburgh, PA 15206
(412) 366-6771

Transplantation Society (TS)
c/o Mary L. Wood
N.E. Deaconess Hospital
185 Pilgrim Road
Boston, MA 02215
(617) 732-8547

United Network for Organ Sharing
  (UNOS)
(800) 24 DONOR

The following list of organizations is categorized according to the specific body part or organ for which information is provided.

LIVER

American Liver Foundation
998 Pompton Avenue
Cedar Grove, NJ 07009
(201) 857-2626
(800) 223-0179

Gutline
American Digestive Disease Society
(301) 652-9293

National Digestive Disease
  Information Clearinghouse
Box NDDIC
Bethesda, MD 20892
(301) 468-6344

EYE

Eye Bank Association of America
  (EBAA)
1511 K Street N.W., Suite 830
Washington, D.C. 20005
(202) 628-4280

Eye-Bank for Sight Restoration
  (EBSR)
210 East 64th Street
New York, NY 10021
(212) 980-6700

Eye Donation Hotline
(301) 638-1818 (Maryland, call
  collect)
(800) 638-1818 (24 hours)

National Eye Institute
National Institutes of Health
Building 31, Room 6A32
Bethesda, MD 20892
(301) 496-5248

EAR

National Temporal Bone Bank
  Program of the Deafness
  Research Foundation

Massachusetts Eye & Ear Infirmary
243 Charles Street
Boston, MA 02114
(617) 523-7900

Eastern and National Center
Massachusetts Eye & Ear Infirmary
243 Charles Street
Boston, MA 02114
(617) 523-7900, ext. 2711

Midwestern Center
University of Minnesota
Box 396—Mayo Clinic
Minneapolis, MN 55455
(612) 373-5466

A Southern Center
Baylor College of Medicine
Neurosurgery Center
Room A523
Houston, TX 77030
(713) 790-5470

Western Center
University of California
School of Medicine
31–24 Rehabilitation Center
Los Angeles, CA 90024
(213) 825-4710

HEART

American Heart Association
7320 Greenville Avenue
Dallas, TX 75231
(214) 750-5300

International Association for Heart
  Transplantation
435 North Michigan Avenue
Suite 177
Chicago, IL 60611
(312) 644-0828

National Heart, Lung, and
  Blood Institute
National Institutes of Health
9000 Rockville Pike
Building 31, Room 4A21
Bethesda, MD 20892
(301) 496-4236

KIDNEY

American Kidney Fund
7315 Wisconsin Avenue
Bethesda, MD 20814
(301) 986-1444
(800) 638-8299
(800) 492-8361 (in Maryland)

National Association of Patients on
  Hemodialysis and
  Transplantation, Inc.
150 Nassau Street
New York, NY 10038
(212) 619-2727

The National Kidney Foundation
2 Park Avenue
New York, NY 10016
(212) 889-2210

BRAIN TISSUE

The Parkinson's
  Disease Foundation
Columbia University
  Medical Center
650 168th Street
New York NY 10032
(212) 923-4700

The National Institute of Neurological and Communicative Diseases and Stroke supports the following brain tissue specimen banks. For information, call or write to:

Dr. Wallace W. Tourtellotte,
  Director
Human Neurospecimen Bank
VA Wadsworth Hospital Center
Los Angeles, CA 90037
(213) 824-4307 or 478-3711
  (24 hours; call collect)

Dr. Edward D. Bird, Director
Brain Tissue Resource Center
McLean Hospital
115 Mill Street
Belmont, MA 02178(617) 855-2400
  (24 hours; call collect)

For further information regarding brain tissue and brain disorders, call or write to:

Parkinson's Educational
  Program USA
1800 Park Newport, Suite 302
Newport Beach, CA 92660
(714) 640-0218
(800) 344-7872

American Association of Tissue
  Banks
1117 North 19th St., Suite 402
Arlington, VA 22209

LUNG

Lung Hotline
(800) 222-LUNG
(303) 398-1477 (in Colorado,
  Monday–Friday, 8:30 A.M.–
  5:30 P.M.

American Lung Association
National Headquarters
1740 Broadway
New York, NY 10019
(212) 315-8700

APPENDIX 2:

How to Become an Organ Donor

If you are 18 years of age or older and of sound mind, you may become an organ donor. If you are under 18 but would still like to become an organ donor, you must have the consent of your parents or guardian. Becoming an organ donor is a decision not to be taken lightly, so it is recommended that you discuss your wishes with family members before making a final decision. In the event of your death, your parents or spouse will have the final say over whether or not your organs are donated, so letting them know your feelings regarding donation in advance will avoid their having to make an agonizing decision during that stressful time.

To become a potential donor, all that you must do is fill out an organ-donor card, which may be obtained through almost any organ bank (such as those listed in the "For More Information" appendix in this book) or by writing to the American Council on Transplantation, P.O. Box 9999, Washington, DC, 20016. The card must be signed by yourself and two witnesses and is considered a legal document.

Some states also provide an opportunity to indicate on your driver's license your wish to be an organ donor. If this is the case in your state, simply check off the box indicating your choice. If you are listed as an organ donor on your driver's license, it is unnecessary to obtain an organ-donor card.

If you have not yet made up your mind to become an organ donor or have decided against it, there is the option of donating blood. Blood can be donated at your local hospital or blood bank in a simple, relatively painless, completely safe procedure. For more information about blood donation, contact your local Red Cross.

FURTHER READING

Barnette, Martha, and the Schroeder family. *The Bill Schroeder Story.* New York: William Morrow, 1987.

Calne, Roy. *The Gift of Life.* New York: Basic Books, 1970.

Clark, Matt, et al. "The New Era of Transplants." *New Scientist* 166 (January 1982).

Davidson, Bill, and the Coleman family. *Gary Coleman: Medical Miracle.* New York: Coward, McCann, Geoghegan, 1981.

Dossick, Philip. *Transplant: A Family Chronicle.* New York: Viking, 1978.

Facklam, Margery and Howard Facklam. *Spare Parts for People.* San Diego: Harcourt Brace Jovanovich, 1987.

Fox, Renee C. *The Courage to Fail.* Chicago: University of Chicago Press, 1974.

Gabriel, Roger, M.D. *A Patient's Guide to Dialysis and Transplantation.* Hingham, MA: Kluwer Boston, 1983.

Gohlke, Mary. *I'll Take Tomorrow.* New York: M. Evans, 1985.

Jarvik, Roger K. "The Total Artificial Heart." *Scientific American* (January 1981): 74-80.

Leinwald, Gerald. *Transplants: Today's Medical Miracles.* New York: Franklin, 1985.

Longmore, Donald. *Spare-part Surgery.* Garden City, NY: Doubleday, 1968.

Madison, Arnold. *Transplanted and Artificial Body Organs.* New York: Bedford Books, 1981.

Metos, Thomas H. *Artificial Humans.* New York: Messner, 1985.

Moore, Francis D. *Give and Take.* Garden City, NY: Doubleday, 1964.

Mowbray, A. Q. *The Transplant.* New York: McKay, 1974.

Nolen, William A. *Spare Parts for the Human Body.* New York: Random House, 1971.

Pekkanen, John. *Donor.* Boston: Little, Brown, 1986.

Poole, Victoria. *Thursday's Child.* Boston: Little, Brown, 1980.

Thornwald, Jurgen. *The Patients.* New York: Harcourt Brace Jovanovich, 1971.

Wingerson, Lois. "The Advance of Organ Transplants." *New Scientist* 166 (January 1982).

GLOSSARY

adrenal glands two small, triangular organs near the kidney that secrete hormones essential to proper nervous-system and organ functions

AIDS acquired immune deficiency syndrome; an acquired defect in the immune system, thought to be caused by a virus (HIV) and spread through blood or sexual contact; leaves people vulnerable to certain, often fatal infections and cancers

allograft "other graft"; transplant from one human being to another

anencephalic having congenital brain damage characterized by partial or complete absence of the cranial vault with cerebral hemispheres completely missing or reduced to small masses attached to the base of the skull

anesthesiologist a physician trained to give anesthetic substances and to monitor heart function and breathing during surgery

anesthetic a substance that causes complete or partial loss of physical sensation

antibiotic a substance produced by or derived from a microorganism and able in solution to inhibit or kill another microorganism; used to combat infection caused by microorganisms, bacteria

antibody a protein made by the body's immune system to combat bacteria, virus, or other foreign substances

antigen a bacteria, virus, or other substance foreign to the body that causes the immune system to produce antibodies

antiseptic a substance that stops the growth of disease-causing bacteria and is used to prevent infection

aplastic anemia a defect in which the bone marrow is depleted of blood-cell-forming tissue, due to exposure to radiation or toxic chemicals in some cases, and to unknown causes in others

artificial heart a mechanical device implanted in the recipient that assumes the function of pumping blood through the circulatory system

autograft a graft of tissue derived from another site in or on the body of the organism receiving it

bacteria unicellular organisms that lack a distinct nuclear membrane; some cause diseases that can be treated with antibiotics such as penicillin

biopsy removal of a small piece of tissue or organ so that it may be examined under a microscope to see if disease is present; after a transplant is done, the tissue or organ sample is checked for signs of the body's immune system rejecting the organ

bone marrow blood-cell-producing tissue inside the bone that manufactures red blood cells and some types of white blood cells

bone-marrow aspiration the process by which red blood cells are extracted from the bone marrow through a long, thin needle

brain death an irreversible condition in which the brain stops functioning while the heart continues to beat

cadaver organ an organ removed from a dead body or from the body of a person who has suffered brain death

cell any one of the minute protoplasmic masses that make up organized tissue, consisting of a nucleus that is surrounded by cytoplasm; a cell is the fundamental structural and functional unit of living organisms

chronic having to do with a disease that persists over a long period of time

clone one or a group of genetically identical cells, organisms, or plants derived by vegetative reproduction from a single parent

congenital involving a condition present at birth

cornea the thin transparent membrane in the front part of the eye; it protects the inner tissues of the eye

cyclosporine a drug that helps to prevent rejection of transplanted organs by slowing down the body's immune system

cystic fibrosis an inherited disease that causes abnormalities in gland secretions, including sweat and saliva, and a thick mucus that can block parts of the lungs, pancreas, sweat glands, and digestive system; eventually it destroys the lungs

diabetes diabetes mellitus; a disease characterized by the body's inability to produce the amount of insulin required to metabolize sugar; although predisposition to the disease is genetically determined, other factors, such as obesity or stress, may contribute to its onset

dialysis a procedure for removing waste products from the blood by filtering the blood through a mechanical membrane; used in cases of kidney failure

DNA deoxyribonucleic acid; genetic material composed of paired nitrogenous bases that contains certain codes for an organism's inherited characteristics; most genes and chromosomes are made of DNA

donor a person who consents to have his or her organs used for transplantation purposes

genes complex units of chemical material contained within the chromosomes of the cells; genes are responsible for inherited traits such as gender or eye color

graft living tissue moved from one place to another on a person's body, or from one person to another person

heart-lung machine a device used to replace the functions of the heart and lungs during surgery

HLA human leukocyte antigen; used to test tissue type to determine if rejection-provoking cells of organ donor are similar to those of recipient

host one who receives a transplanted organ; the recipient

immune system the body's mechanism for combating viruses, bacteria, and other outside threats; composed of various types of white blood cell, including phagocytes, which consume bacteria, and lymphocytes, which produce antibodies

implant material inserted into the body, especially synthetic organs

informed consent permission from the patient to do a test or procedure, given after the patient understands what is to be done, why, what benefits might be obtained, and what might go wrong

insulin a protein hormone produced in the pancreas and important to the regulation of the blood-sugar level; lack of this hormone may lead to diabetes, in which large amounts of sugar are present in the blood and urine because the body is not able to metabolize it; the condition may be treated by injections of insulin

insulin pump a battery-driven pump worn externally by a diabetic that automatically injects premeasured doses of insulin; pumps may also be implanted and monitored by an external computer

intravenous(IV) the process of giving fluid or medication through a tube inserted into a vein

kidneys either of the two bean-shaped organs that cleanse and filter blood, excreting the end products of body metabolism in the form of urine

lens the part of the eye that allows sight to be focused

leukemia cancer of the blood-forming organs; causes the bone marrow to produce deformed blood cells

leukocyte a white blood cell used by the body to destroy invading bacteria

liver a large complex gland of the body; located in the top part of the abdominal cavity, its functions are fat digestion, metabolism, vitamin processing, and neutralization of poisons such as alcohol

lupus erythematosus an inflammatory disease that damages body tissue; antibodies in a person's immune system attack the body's own substances, causing cell and tissue damage, destroying immunological tolerance, and causing problems with the body's connective tissue; may affect the kidneys, joints, and the heart; it is possibly triggered by exposure to ultraviolet radiation, drugs, or foreign proteins in the body

lymph node one of a number of small swellings found at intervals along the lymphatic system

lymphocyte a variety of white blood cell involved in immunity; includes B-lymphocytes and T-lymphocytes

lymphoma Any malignant tumor of the lymph nodes, excluding Hodgkin's disease; victims suffer weight loss, fever, and sweating

metabolism the process by which substances within a living organism are chemically broken down in order to utilize useful energy

monoclonal antibody a laboratory-made antibody that is used to slow the rejection of a transplanted organ while leaving the rest of the person's immune system intact; its usefulness generally lasts for 10 days

myopathy a muscle disorder that causes severe weakness

Novocain a trade name for procaine, a local anesthetic, usually administered by injection

organ a part of the body made up of tissues specialized to perform a certain function; the heart is an organ whose function is to pump blood

organ bank a place equipped to store donated organs until they are transplanted, or to arrange for the donation of organs for transplant

pancreas an organ composed of cells that secrete enzymes carried in the pancreatic juice for digestive purposes, and to turn food into energy

Parkinson's disease a disease of the nervous system in which muscle movement slows and tremors occur; the disease, usually found in the elderly, is caused by a deficiency of dopamine, a chemical in the brain that transmits impulses between nerves

peripheral vascular disease the blockage of vessels in the legs by fatty deposits and hardening of the arteries

prednisone a medication used to slow down the body's immune system and thus prevent rejection of a transplanted organ; may cause bloating and distortion of the facial features

recombinant DNA part of a gene that has been broken up and put back together in a new form

serum clear fluid that remains when the red blood cells are removed from the blood

sickle-cell anemia an inherited blood disease in which malformed red blood cells are produced; may cause reduced oxygen delivery to some tissue and organs, or abnormal blood flow due to the odd shape of the blood cells

steroid any naturally occuring fat-soluble organic compound, including the male sex-hormone androgen, the female sex-hormone estrogen, and progesterone; synthetic steroids have been produced for therapeutic purposes

Tay-Sachs disease an inherited genetic disease that results from a metabolic abnormality, which causes fatty deposits to build up in the brain, destruction of the central nervous system, brain damage, and early death; the disease occurs most often in those of Jewish and Mediterranean descent

T-helper cell a cell that signals other lymphocytes to attack invading cells or chemical structures foreign to the body

tissue a collection of cells that act together to perform a specific function in the body; aggregations of tissue constitute organs

tissue biopsy a procedure during which a small piece of an organ is removed from the body through a long hollow needle and its cells examined microscopically; used after transplantation to check for signs of rejection

tissue typing a test performed to determine whether the tissues of a prospective organ donor and organ recipient are similar enough to allow for a successful transplant

INDEX

Adrenal gland, 90
Adrenal-to-brain grafts, 90
Aguayo, Albert, 89
AIDS (acquired immune deficiency
        syndrome), 54
Allografts, 29, 30, 33, 34
Alzheimer's disease, 90
American Academy of Pediatrics, 76
American Medical Association, 39
Anencephalic infants, 84–86
Animal-to-human grafts, 20, 83–84
Antibiotics, 25
Antibodies, 22, 48
Antigens, 43, 48
Aplastic anemia, 24, 48
Artificial heart, 15, 54
Artificial inner-ear device, 91
Artificial skin, 32, 91
Autografts, 30, 31–32, 33

Baby Fae, 83
Bailey, Leonard, 83
Barnard, Christiaan, 14, 25
Baronio, Giuseppe, 19
Baxter, Charles, 26
Bell, Eugene, 32
Belzer, Folkert O., 92
Blood transfusions, 22
Blood-vessel transplants, 32–33
Bone banks, 30
Bone marrow aspiration, 33
Bone-marrow transplants, 25, 33–34,
        43
Bone transplants, 14, 20, 29–30
Borel, Jean, 49, 52

Burke, John, 32
Burnet, MacFarlane, 22

Calne, R. Y., 49
Cambridge University, 49, 88
Carrel, Alexis, 20–21
Cell transplants, 89–90
Chernobyl, 25
Chimera, 17
Cloning, 26
Coleman, Gary, 35
Corneal transplants, 14, 28–30
Cosmas and Damian, 17
Cyclosporine, 25–26, 34, 35, 49, 52–
        53, 54, 64, 71, 72
    cost of, 53
Cystic fibrosis, 90

Dameshek, William, 25
Darvall, Denise, 14
Diabetes, 15, 48, 89, 91
Dialysis, 14, 28, 35, 36, 54, 66–68,
        70, 71,
    peritoneal, 35
DiMaggio, Donald, 60
DNA (deoxyribonucleic acid), 90–91
Dopamine, 90

Electrocautery, 58
Epilepsy, 90
Escherichia coli, 48
Eye banks, 13, 28

Federal Health Care Finance Administration, 82–83
Fiske, Charles, 75–77
Fiske, Jamie, 75–76
Food and Drug Administration, 52
Freed, W. J., 89

General anesthesia, 19–20, 29, 57
 first use of, 19–20
Glycosaminoglycan, 32
Guthrie, Charles, 20–21

Heart-lung machine, 59
Heart-lung transplants, 14, 36–37, 45, 54
Heart transplants, 14, 25, 36–37, 40, 45, 52, 53, 55–60, 83–84
 cost of, 82
 cyclosporine and, 26
 on a dog, 21
 on infants, 83–84
 myopathy and, 36
Herpes simplex, 47
Holman, Emile, 21–22
Human leukocyte antigens (HL-A), 43
Hume, David, 22
Hunter, John, 19

Immune system, 20, 21–22, 33, 47–53
 and drugs, 49, 52–53, 88–89
 rejection by, 22–25, 42, 53–54
Implants, 14–15, 28–29, 88–91
Insulin, 15, 89, 91
Insulin pump, 15, 91
IV, 57

Kennedy, Edward, 76
Kidney/pancreas transplants, 25
Kidney transplants, 13–14, 16, 22–23, 25, 35, 40, 43, 45, 53, 61, 62, 89

a case history, 65–74
 on cats, 21
 cost, 82
 effect of cyclosporine on, 53

Landsteiner, Karl, 22
La Raza Medical Center, 90
L-dopa, 90
Lens implants, 28–29, 30
Leukemia, 25, 33
Leukocytes, 43
Lister, Joseph, 20
Liver transplants, 14, 25, 26, 35–36, 44–45, 54
 cost of, 82
 success rate of, 36
Loma Linda University Medical Center, 83, 85
Lymphocytes, 48, 50
Lymphoma, 53

McGill University, 89
Madroza, Ignazio, 90
Massachusetts General Hospital, 19
Massachusetts Institute of Technology, 32
Medawar, Peter, 22, 25
Medicaid, 46
Medicare, 46
Medinacelli, Louis de, 89
Milstein, Cesar, 88
Monoclonal antibodies, 88–89
Morton, William T. G., 19
Muscle transplants, 20

National Institute of Mental Health, 89
Nerve transplants, 89
Nitrogen mustard, 48
Nobel Prize, 22, 88
Novocain, 68

Omnibus Budget Act of 1986, 46
O'Neill, Thomas, 76

On the Surgery of Mutilation by Grafting Techniques (Tagliacozzi), 18
Organ banks, 28–29
Organogenesis, 32
Organ transplants
    antirejection drugs, 25–26, 27, 35, 40, 42, 43, 48–49, 52–53, 54, 55, 59–60, 62, 64, 71–72, 88
        side effects of, 53, 62, 64, 71–72, 88. *See also* Cyclosporine
    blood-typing, 22–24, 42
    effects of the immune system, 20, 21–22, 24–25, 42, 47–50, 54
    emotional health, 40, 55–56, 61–65, 71–73
    ethics, 16, 75–86
        and anencephalic babies, 84–86
        and sale of organs, 81–82
        and use of publicity, 75–78
    finances, 16, 53, 56, 64–65, 82–83
    graft-versus-host reaction, 33–34
    history, 14–16, 17–26
    legality, 16, 44, 46, 78, 79, 80, 82, 86
        and brain death, 44, 79–80
    rejection reaction, 21–26, 29, 30, 32, 33–34, 35, 37–38, 42, 47–54, 59–60, 62, 69, 83, 89
    religion, 19, 80
    selection of donors and recipients, 16, 39–46, 55–57, 62, 69, 75–82, 85–86
        and cadaver organs, 44, 62, 92
        and live donations, 43
        and twins, 23–24, 33
        and use of computer databanks, 41, 46, 56, 78
    size of organ, 41
    supply of organs, 16, 44–46, 62, 82, 92
    surgery and surgical techniques, 14–16, 17–21, 25, 26, 28, 29, 36–38, 39–40, 57–60, 89–90
        and anaesthesia, 19–20, 25, 29, 57
        and blood vessels, 20, 32–33, 59, 66–67

    and infants, 83–86
    and infections, 19, 20, 25, 40, 44–45, 47, 48, 55, 56, 57, 59–60, 71
    survival rates, 13–14, 26, 30, 34–37, 52–53, 89
    tissue typing, 25–26, 42–43, 56
Orthoclone OKT3, 88–89
Ortho Pharmaceutical Corporation, 88

Pancreas transplants, 89
Parkinson, James, 90
Parkinson's disease, 90
Peripheral vascular disease, 33
Peritoneal dialysis, 35
Peter Brent Brigham Hospital, 22
Plasma, 58
Prednisone, 53, 71
    side effects of, 53
Pulmonary vein, 59

Radiation, 24, 25, 48
Receptor cells, 50
Reitz, Bruce, 26
Rejection, 21–26, 29, 30, 32, 33–34, 35, 37–38, 42, 47–54, 59–60, 62, 69, 83, 89
Reverdin, Jaques, 19

Sandimmune, 53. *See also* Cyclosporine
Sandoz Pharmaceuticals, 49, 53
Schwartz, Robert, 25
Shumway, Norman, 14, 26, 52
Sickle-cell anemia, 90
6-mercaptopurine, 48
Skin grafts, 18–19, 20, 21–22, 30–32
    burn injuries, 31–32
    flap grafts, 31–32
    full-thickness autograft, 31–32
    split-thickness autograft, 32
Southard, James, 92
Stanford University Medical Center, 14, 26, 52
Starzl, Thomas, 25, 26, 78

Steroids, 48, 64
Subcutaneous arteriovenous shunt, 66
Substantia nigra, 90
Synthetic body parts, 14, 91
  Dacron, 33, 67
  Gore-Tex, 67
  Teflon, 33, 67

Tagliacozzi, Gaspare, 18–19
Task Force on Transplantation, 77
Tay-Sachs disease, 90
T-cell antigen receptor, 89
Terasaki, Paul I., 25
T-helper cell, 49
Thyroid glands, 32
Tissue biopsy, 48
Tissue typing, 25–26, 42–43, 56
T-lymphocyte, 89
Transplant coordinator, 44
Typing serum, 43

Uniform Anatomical Gift Act, 78–79
Uniform Donor Card, 78–79

University of Baltimore, 26
University of California-Los Angeles (UCLA), 25
University of Chicago, 20
University of Pittsburgh, 25
University of Texas, 26
University of Wisconsin, 92
UNOS (United Network for Organ Sharing), 46, 78
U.S. Congress, 77
U.S. government, 46, 78

Vena cava, 59

Washansky, Louis, 14, 25
White, David, 49
Winner, Brenda and Michael, 84–85
Winter, David, 53

X rays, 24–25

Yannis, Ioannis, 32

PICTURE CREDITS

American Council on Transplantation: p. 41; AP/Wide World Photos: pp. 13, 24, 30, 31, 34, 42, 52, 55, 56, 57, 59, 60, 61, 84, 87, 88; The Bettmann Archive: pp. 18, 21, 23; Courtesy of The Eye-Bank for Sight Restoration: p. 28; Chaplain William Hinton/Loma Linda University Medical Center: p. 63; John Messina/Rapho/Photo Researchers, Inc.: pp. 27, 69, 70; Jeff Mettesheim & Associates/American Liver Foundation of Wisconsin: p. 77; Robert Rearick/Loma Linda University Medical Center: pp. 82, 91; Reuters/Bettmann Newsphotos: p. 17; Sandoz Pharmaceuticals: pp. 47, 73; United Network for Organ Sharing: p. 39; UPI/Bettmann Newsphotos: pp. 15, 37, 45, 58, 64, 75, 81, 85AA; Original illustrations by Gary Tong: pp. 51, 66, 67

Mary Kittredge, a former associate editor of the medical journal *Respiratory Care*, is a free-lance writer of nonfiction and fiction. She is certified as a respiratory-care technician by the American Association for Respiratory Therapy and has been a member of the respiratory-care staff at Yale–New Haven Hospital and Medical Center since 1972.

Ms. Kittredge was educated at Trinity College, Hartford, and the University of California Medical Center, San Francisco. She is the author of *The Respiratory System* and *Prescription & Over-the-Counter Drugs* in the Chelsea House ENCYCLOPEDIA OF HEALTH series, and of young-adult biographies *Marc Antony, Frederick the Great,* and *Jane Addams.* Her writing awards include the Ruell Crompton Tuttle Essay Prize and the Mystery Writers of America Robert L. Fish Award for best first short-mystery fiction of 1986.

Dale C. Garell, M.D., is medical director of California Childrens Services, Department of Health Services, County of Los Angeles. He is also clinical professor in the Department of Pediatrics and Family Medicine at the University of Southern California School of Medicine and Visiting associate clinical professor of maternal and child health at the University of Hawaii School of Public Health. From 1963 to 1974, he was medical director of the Division of Adolescent Medicine at Children's Hospital in Los Angeles. Dr. Garell has served as president of the Society for Adolescent Medicine, chairman of the youth committee of the American Academy of Pediatrics, and as a forum member of the White House Conference on Children (1970) and White House Conference on Youth (1971). He has also been a member of the editorial board of the *American Journal of Diseases of Children.*

C. Everett Koop, M.D., Sc.D., is Surgeon General, Deputy Assistant Secretary for Health, and Director of the Office of International Health of the U.S. Public Health Service. A pediatric surgeon with an international reputation, he was previously surgeon-in-chief of Children's Hospital of Philadelphia and professor of pediatric surgery and pediatrics at the University of Pennsylvania. Dr. Koop is the author of more than 175 articles and books on the practice of medicine. He has served as surgery editor of the *Journal of Clinical Pediatrics* and editor-in-chief of the *Journal of Pediatric Surgery.* Dr. Koop has received nine honorary degrees and numerous other awards, including the Denis Brown Gold Medal of the British Association of Paediatric Surgeons, the William E. Ladd Gold Medal of the American Academy of Pediatrics, and the Copernicus Medal of the Surgical Society of Poland. He is a Chevalier of the French Legion of Honor and a member of the Royal College of Surgeons, London.